History of Rome

A Captivating Guide to Roman History, Starting from the Legend of Romulus and Remus through the Roman Republic, Byzantium, Medieval Period, and Renaissance to Modern History

Free Bonus from Captivating History (Available for a Limited time)

Hi History Lovers!

Now you have a chance to join our exclusive history list so you can get your first history ebook for free as well as discounts and a potential to get more history books for free! Simply visit the link below to join.

Captivatinghistory.com/ebook

Also, make sure to follow us on Facebook, Twitter and Youtube by searching for Captivating History.

Contents

Introduction

The first settlers of the hills overlooking the Tiber River progressed quickly. From this unidentified culture, a city rose, a city that would become famous relatively quickly and soon rule half the known world. These first settlers eventually conquered most of Europe, the Near East, and North Africa. They would control these areas throughout the centuries.

Rome started as a kingdom, thrived as a republic, conquered vast territories when it was an empire, and became the Holy City during the Middle Ages. Even today, Rome continues to intrigue us with its rich history, architecture, art, literature, religion, laws, and language. The abundant archaeological findings of Rome and its surrounding are but a fragment of what the city once was. Nevertheless, it is enough to engage us, tickle our imagination, and satisfy our thirst for knowledge. Unfortunately, human carelessness destroyed much of the city during the bombings of World War II, and many precious artifacts and evidence are forever lost. There are aspects of Rome, such as its social structure, politics, and strategies, we will never fully understand, but we must be thankful for the glimpses into Rome's past that we have.

The history of Rome is an ongoing dialogue, as archaeologists continue to bring forward new evidence, even from far away. China provided evidence that the first Roman delegation visited its shores as early as 166 CE. This made people realize that the current knowledge we have on Rome isn't fixed and absolute. There is more to find on the Eternal City, and it may yet surprise us. The importance of Rome cannot be argued. Its history is not the history of Italy or its people. Rome is a part of the foundation of Europe, just as Athens is. Without it, the world as we know it today wouldn't exist.

Through the Middle Ages, Rome led humanity to new heights. It sacrificed itself to produce a new empire to dominate the world. Even though it was located far from Rome, the Byzantine Empire was her child, and the history of Constantinople cannot be separated from that of Rome. The struggles between the two cities that occurred during medieval times remind us of those between a parent and a child. It was only natural for Constantinople to wish to separate itself. Unfortunately, this brought strong divisions between the people, as the Great Schism separated the Catholics from the Orthodox Christians. This division persists, even though we are once more united through the simple human compassion for each other.

Rome almost fell into oblivion during the Late Middle Ages, but the Renaissance brought it back from the brink of death. Popes worked tirelessly to restore the former glory of the Eternal City and brought various artists and scholars to Rome, who gave their soul to the city. But even then, during its peak of beauty and power, Rome wasn't without controversy. This richness brought corruption, a leisurely life for the clergy, and the harsh Inquisition to fight some of the greatest minds of the time. Concepts such as heliocentrism and the existence of multiple worlds were born during this age, but it was quickly put down by the strict dogmas of the Catholic Church. However, Rome continued to evolve and make progress.

Rome, and Italy in general, did not have a great entrance into contemporary history, as they promoted a dictator, Benito Mussolini, to rule. Under his leadership, Italy joined World War II as one of the Axis powers. Italians fought and died for Germany and their Nazi ideology, ideas in which they never believed. But the spirit of the Italian people couldn't be crushed, and there was a light at the end of the tunnel. Under new leadership, Italy managed to switch sides and become one of the victors in the devastating war. Unfortunately, Rome couldn't escape the bombings, which left scars on the Eternal City that can be seen today. Some healed quickly, as Europe realized what could be lost and financed the city's reconstruction. But some scars were intentionally left to remind us never to repeat history. After all, it is time to make new history, this time better and brighter. Rome continues as one of the prettiest and culturally richest cities in the world, standing high for us to wonder at its glory and to remind us of our own history. Because, after all, we all have a little bit of ancient Rome in ourselves.

Chapter 1 – The Founding of Rome: Myth and Reality

There are many stories concerning the foundation of the most famous European city. It is human nature to try to explain significant events throughout history. It is the primordial need to know one's ancestry and roots, for it is through this that national pride is developed. The sense of belonging to a community is a natural response by which we ensure our survival. But to create a community, there has to be something that binds people together. When it comes to nations, cities, and states, that is usually a common ancestry.

Rome has a beautiful yet very unusual myth about its foundation, which is believed to be the first history of the city. The archaeological evidence to support this myth doesn't exist, but it is quite normal that history and myth have nothing in common. Still, Romans often choose to believe in the mythological version of their ancestry and the city's foundation than what history has to offer, even though both accounts are equally interesting and intriguing.

The Myth of Romulus and Remus

Sculpture of Romulus and Remus being fed by a she-wolf.

The majority of ancient sources agree that Rome was founded by Romulus and his twin brother Remus. They were the descendants of mythological King Numitor, who ruled in a mythological city of an unknown name in the Alban Hills; some claim the city in question was Alba Longa. But this story begins even before the brothers were born. Numitor was deposed by his brother Amulius. The fate of the king is unknown, but his young daughter, Rhea Silvia, survived the ordeal and was installed as a Vestal Virgin. As the priestess of the goddess Vesta, Rhea was expected to remain chaste, as Amulius wanted no throne pretenders to appear in the future. However, Rhea became pregnant, and she gave birth to twin boys. It is unknown who was the supposed father of her children, but some of the ancient sources mention the god Mars. Amulius immediately ordered the boys to be drowned in the River Tiber, but the river didn't claim their lives. The twins washed ashore at the foot of Palatine Hill, one of the seven hills on which the future city of Rome would lie. There, a she-wolf found the boys, and she nurtured them with her milk after being inspired by the divine. Eventually, the boys were found by a shepherd named Faustulus, who adopted the twins.

The boys grew up herding sheep, and over time, they proved to be capable leaders of the warrior-shepherd band that lived in the region. On one occasion, Romulus and Remus found themselves in their city of birth, unaware of their ancestry. They involved themselves in the dispute between Numitor and his brother Amulius. For this, Remus was imprisoned, while his brother managed to escape. He gathered his band and attacked the city to free his brother. However, while in prison, Remus learned his true identity as the grandson of Numitor. Once he was freed, both Romulus and Remus helped their grandfather reclaim the throne, killing Amulius in the process. The brothers declined to remain in the city, as they felt the need to remain and lead their people. They left the unknown mythical city in the Alban Hills to found their own city.

Romulus and Remus couldn't decide on which of the seven hills to establish the city. Romulus wanted it to be Palatine Hill, where the river had washed them ashore, while Remus wanted Aventine Hill instead. After arguing over the matter, the brothers finally agreed to consult the divines. But Romulus was angry over the petty quarrel, and he murdered his brother to found the city on Palatine Hill. Romulus named the city of Rome after himself. He was the founding father and the first king of the city, although some still remember his brother Remus, and they honor him with the title of founding father as well.

There are many versions of this story, and each one gives a different mythological meaning to it. In some versions, the father of Romulus and Remus was Mars, the god of war. This would explain the later Roman expansion policies and the significance of its military, which was one of the most developed in the world at the time. However, others claim Rhea Silvia was impregnated by a spark from the hearth. As a Vestal Virgin, her obligation was to tend the sacred flame in the temple, and this story gives a domestic narrative to the myth. The hearth is the center of the house, and Vesta is the goddess of the home and family. As founding fathers of Rome, Romulus and Remus needed to be connected with the symbolism of family, which would be a bonding way to unite the Romans into a community.

Another disputed piece of the myth is the she-wolf. Sources refer to her only as *lupa*, which is translated as "she-wolf." But at the time, *lupa* was a term people would use to refer to a prostitute. Scholars today believe that Romulus and Remus were nursed by a local prostitute and that the statue of the she-wolf so well known today has its origin in the Middle Ages. During medieval times, Latin was only used in the Church, and it wasn't the same Latin as the original. It is believed that either the priests didn't know the other meaning of the word *lupa*, or they intentionally changed it to "she-wolf" to remove the existence of sin from the myth about Rome's foundation. But the wolf was a sacred animal to ancient Italic peoples. There was even a tribe, the Hirpini, whose name originates from the ancient Oscan language and means "wolf people." The earliest evidence of the Roman she-wolf represented on comes from the 3rd century BCE, proving that even before the Middle Ages, Rome believed in the legend of Romulus and Remus and their upbringing by a wild beast.

To justify the fratricide in the myth, some versions say that Romulus already built the walls around Palatine Hill and that Remus jumped over and started destroying what his brother had built. This angered Romulus, who killed his brother as punishment for the destruction. This version seems to justify the later belligerent attitude of Rome, a city whose wars and expansions were always justified as responding to the aggression of others. It also represents the will of its people who would defend the walls of the city, even if it meant killing their loved ones, as Romulus himself did. After all, the history of Rome is filled with accounts of betrayal and civil wars where its citizens turned against each other.

The myth of Rome's foundation doesn't end with the fratricide. The gruesome tale continues, as the newly founded city needed citizens. According to the legend, Romulus was a leader of a band of warrior-shepherds, but their number was small. To attract more people, he declared Rome as an asylum city, inviting criminals, runaway slaves, and exiles to join. But no women came. What happened next inspired artists all over the world. The scene is captured in many paintings, engravings, sculptures, and in literary works, both prose and poetry. Romulus organized a religious festival, inviting the neighboring Latins and Sabines to come as guests. Once the male guests were drunk enough, he ordered his men to capture the women, rape them, and take them as their wives. In all the paintings that depict the scene of the kidnapping, Romulus is represented as king standing on a dais and overseeing the violence happening at his feet. In the background, Rome is under construction. This was the first Roman marriage, and its origin is in rape.

How do the violence, rape, and abductions justify the myth of Rome's foundation? As we have seen, all the parts of the myth have a deeper meaning behind it that appealed to the people of Rome in one way or another. At first glance, this scene is too obscene to serve some higher purpose. But not all scholars agree. One of the earliest Roman historians, Livy, wrote that Romans abducted only unmarried women, as if this would offer some defense. But he also claims that Romulus offered a treaty to his neighbors that would give his citizens the right to marry the daughters of Latins and Sabines. But his treaty was turned down, and it was only then, in an act of desperation, that the people of Rome turned to violence. Again, their actions were justified, as the people of Rome would do anything to secure their survival and continuity.

However, modern scholars believe the abduction of women represents a war prize. The need for a treaty alludes that there was some kind of conflict going on, and the kidnapping and raping of the opponents' women was not an unusual sight in ancient times. But others claim that the violence presented in this scene is nothing else than the description of the earliest model of flirtation. Since humans succumbed to their instincts more often back then, it was sexual and primitive, not consensual, as in modern times.

The myth continues with what is believed to be the first described war between the rivaling Romans and Sabines. The conflict dragged on for years, as the Sabines wouldn't give up on their daughters. In the end, the women saved the day. They entered the battlefield, begging their new husbands and their fathers to stop fighting, for they would rather die than continue without their spouses or fathers. This moment shows the women had made peace with their destiny of becoming proud wives and mothers of Rome. From this day, Rome united with Sabine, and it became one city ruled by joint kings: Romulus and Titus Tatius. But after only three years, the Sabine king was killed in an uprising, and Romulus became the sole king of Rome, reigning for over thirty years.

The myth of Romulus and Remus is just a part of a much larger myth. The history of Rome is older than the twin brothers, and it is described by the famous ancient Roman poet Virgil in his epic poem, the *Aeneid*. This larger myth tells the story of Aeneas, a Trojan who sailed from his home city once it was destroyed by the famous Trojan War. In fact, Aeneas was already known to the public from the Greek myth of Troy and the famous Greek poem *Iliad*, which was written by Homer. Aeneas was already known as the ancestor of the Romans when Virgil took it upon himself to reconstruct the myth. He did it under the command of Emperor Augustus, who wanted to give his rule legitimacy by painting himself as a descendant of the famous Aeneas through his family ties with Gaius Julius Caesar. While he is only a minor character in Homer's epos, Aeneas's story was taken by the Romans, who continued the myth.

After the fall of Troy, the gods commanded Aeneas to flee and find a new home for himself and his men. He stopped in Sicily and Carthage, but these were not good places to inhabit. His travels continued until he landed on the shores of western Italy. There, he was welcomed by Latinus, the king of Latium, whose daughter, Lavinia, Aeneas married. Together, they founded the city of Lavinius, named after his wife. After his death, Aeneas was cleansed of the mortal part of his soul by the gods, and he became a deity known as Jupiter Indiges. His son, Iulus, founded Alba Longa, and he was the ancestor of Romulus and Remus. This myth connects the Romans with the Trojans, giving them a historical narrative on which the founding myth could be built. Proud of their ancestry, ancient Romans finally had something to unite them and give them a national identity of their own.

Archaeological Evidence

If something is historically proven from the founding myth of Rome, it is that the city was founded on an area previously occupied by pastoral settlements. The hills on which Rome lies used to be covered in small villages, who found them appropriate to shelter them from invaders and as the source of food for their herds. The oldest dated village is the one occupying Capitol Hill, and its origins are connected to the 14th century BCE. There are signs of even earlier settlements, which are believed to be Paleolithic and Neolithic, but unfortunately, they are covered under the layers of newer ruins. Excessive and careful excavations are needed, but for now, the archaeological value of the Roman ruins is too great to be disturbed.

The first permanent settlement in the vicinity of today's Rome is dated at around 1000 BCE. The possibility of earlier ones exists, but since there is no appropriate way of performing deeper excavations without ruining the sites, we can only speculate if they were permanent or not. The cremation graves found in Rome are very similar to the ones discovered in the Alban Hills, Pratica di Mare (the famous Aeneas's Lavinium), and the Sabine country. These first settlements belonged to what scholars call *cultura laziale*, or the "Latial culture." The only evidence of this culture is the graves and their unique burial rites. The graves in the vicinity of Rome contain everyday items next to an urn with the deceased's ashes. The first phase of the Latial culture lasted between 1000 and 900 BCE, but nothing is known about its community. The earliest discovered settlements of the Latial culture have been dated to the beginning of the Iron Age, which corresponds to the second phase of the Latial culture.

The villages discovered on the hills of Rome were very small in the beginning. Based on the number of gravesites, they couldn't have had more than 100 inhabitants. The largest one was on Palatine Hill, and it is believed that it attracted people from other settlements because it was an important trade center. The historical consensus is that Rome grew gradually and spread from Palatine Hill to neighboring hills. Because of this, we cannot pinpoint the exact year of the city's foundation. Even the ancient Romans couldn't tell the year, but they did celebrate April 21ˢᵗ as the date of the city's birth. The importance of Palatine Hill has already been described in the myth of Romulus and Remus, as it was one of the chosen sites to build the city. But why exactly were these hills chosen? From an archaeological aspect, they do provide a perfect geographical zone for a settlement. They are near to the sea, and the River Tiber acts as a perfect source of fresh water. The hills themselves act as a natural defense against both natural disasters and possible enemies, but they are positioned in such a way that they are at the center of a crossroads. The old Roman phrase, "All roads lead to Rome," is evidence of this.

The first settlers came to the vicinity of Rome from the Alban Hills. The pastoral people turned into farmers, and they needed more fertile lands of the Tiber River Valley. But who exactly were the first Italians, and what was their pre-Roman background? Italy always had a diverse landscape, which, in pre-Roman times, was occupied with many diverse peoples. The country itself was a patchwork of little kingdoms with different people, cultures, and languages. Unfortunately, we don't have much evidence about all the societies that made up pre-Roman Italy. However, there is a big difference between material items originating in the Late Bronze Age compared with items from the Early Iron Age. It seems there was a cultural unity during the last years of the Bronze Age. But suddenly, that unity disappeared and was replaced with the vast diversity of the Iron Age. Scholars don't have an explanation for this occurrence yet, but it is believed this is the point when the history of the Italian people begins.

During the Iron Age, the culture of the Italian people can be divided into two groups: Northern, which practiced cremation burial rights, and the rest of Italy, which practiced inhumation (burying corpses). However, the important thing to remember is that cultural classification doesn't necessarily mean different nations. One nation can have different customs and rites yet have the same society and culture as another. The burial custom is a measure for early cultural classification for the simple reason that tombs are our main source of information. There are no settlements discovered for these early cultures that would give us an insight into their daily lives.

The Northern crematory culture can be further divided into smaller cultural groups, each with distinctive characteristics. To the far north, near the Alps, the Golasecca culture emerged with its distinctive warrior elite class. In the area of the Po Valley, the Este culture emerged with their fine bronze items. The most important that pertains to Rome is the Villanovan culture, which originated from the Emilia-Romagna region. It is named after the excavation site near Bologna. The most prominent characteristic of the

Villanovan culture is the burial site found there. The ashes of the deceased were placed in a biconical urn and sealed with a lid that resembled a helmet or a bowl. A localized variation of this burial rite occurs in Latium. There, the culture used to be called the "Southern Villanovan," but it now is known as the Latial culture.

However, the Latial culture did not originate from the Villanovan culture. It was influenced by the Northern culture, but its origins can be found in the Apennine culture of central Italy. It is believed the pastoral people, who came down from the Apennine Mountains to the fertile valley of the Tiber River, adopted some of the burial rites of the Villanovans, although they spoke different languages and probably had a different ethnicity. Again, not much is known about the everyday life of the Latiums, as the only evidence we have is their burial grounds. It is known they spoke a proto-Latin language, which allows us to recognize them as people who identified as one of the Latin tribes inhabiting the Alban Hills. The tribal self-consciousness of these Roman ancestors occurred during the reign of the Alban kings and the foundation of the Roman Kingdom.

Chapter 2 – The Kingdom of Rome

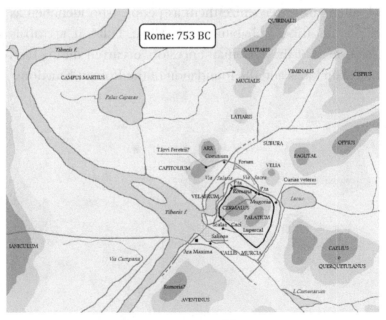

Rome in 753 BCE

During the late 8th century BCE, the villages on top of the hills started to merge and form one large nucleated settlement. Scholars call this phase of urbanization a proto-urban phenomenon. The settlements grew both in the number of people and their prosperity, but they were not yet urban centers. Gradually, they would develop into city-states, what the Greeks used to call poleis (singular: polis). The largest number of these proto-urban settlements has been discovered in ancient Etruria, today's Tuscany, in central Italy. The Etruscans were not Latin; in fact, they originated from Asia Minor. But they were the most influential society in Italy. Their power spread from central regions to the south, reaching even Sicily. The Etruscans were the first neighbors of Rome, and as such, they influenced early Roman culture. Some Roman kings were Etruscans, and they were responsible for spreading Greek influence all over Italy.

Etruria had its own language, which was commonly used until at least the 1st century BCE when it was replaced with Latin. Even though there are thousands of Etruscan documents and texts at our disposal today, we are still struggling to understand the language. It is written in some form of Greek, and it was adapted to suit their language. However, the language is completely unknown; it has no cognates, and it is not Indo-European. The texts written in the Etruscan language can be broadly understood, but the nuances of its grammar are complicated and not yet deciphered. Luckily, some texts are written in both Etruscan and Latin, confirming the theory that these two peoples were connected and influenced each other.

Rome started showing the first signs of urbanization while under the influence of Etruria in the late 8th and early 7th century BCE. By then, this great city was just a collection of large huts that were built seemingly without order or planning. But the big change occurred during the 7th century with the rise of the aristocratic class. Aside from the large newly-built tombs, which were often placed outside of the main necropolis, the evidence for the emerging elite can also be found in the countryside, where large estates were built. Both tombs and country homes of the aristocracy were of monumental size, often decorated richly to display the prosperity of the family. With the rise of the aristocracy, the urban planning of the settlements began, allowing for the development of the first cities to occur.

Rome has the earliest evidence of such urban planning and development in Italy. The first forum was built during the mid-7th century when the huts around the Via Sacra were demolished to make a gathering place, the first public square. Around the same time, permanent houses appeared, replacing the huts as living quarters. The new houses were built of stone, and they had tiled roofs. Similar buildings were found at Palatine Hill, but they were dated to the early 6th century. The earliest dated public building was found at the eastern end of the Forum, the so-called Regia ("Royal House"). It is believed this building served as the king's residence; later, during the Roman Republic, it became a shrine to the god Mars. The first Senate House was built at the opposite end of the Forum, and it is dated to 600 BCE. The first temple was dedicated to Vesta, and it is also considered to date from around 600 BCE. The items found in the temple were of both Etruscan and Greek origin, confirming the Romans already had a strong connection with other ethnic groups in Italy. While the Greek items could have been imported through Etruria, which traded overseas, Italy also had its first Greek colony in the mid-8th century BCE.

All this evidence paints a large picture of Rome's urbanization. From a primitive settlement to an organized city, Rome developed very fast. The archaeological discoveries are further supported by written evidence, which mainly describes the public work done by the kings. This "urban revolution" marks the beginning of Roman history. The city-state of Rome was a monarchy, and it was ruled by a king who had ultimate power over the people.

The Monarchy

The archaeological evidence that would confirm the existence of kings is sparse. Only one inscription includes the word "king" ("RECEI") in the early form of the Latin language. Unfortunately, the inscription as a whole is incomprehensible, as a large part of it is missing. It is believed that the inscription dates from the early 6th century BCE, although it is hard to precisely determine the date. The text was at first confused as a Greek inscription until scholars realized the language is a form of very early Latin, written in letters similar to ancient Greek. Nevertheless, archaeologists concluded that the "RECEI" form is a dative case, or an indirect object. Therefore, it is translated as "to the king" or "for the king."

This archaeological evidence was enough to confirm what the written evidence already exposed: Rome was ruled by kings for the first two and a half centuries of its existence. The Roman historian Livy notes a sequence of six kings who ruled after Romulus. To historians, they are known as the "seven legendary kings of Rome," as there is no archaeological evidence of their existence. Livy wrote colorful stories about the heroism and the great deeds of the kings. He also noted their achievements, which served to develop the politics and everyday life of Roman people.

The first of the seven legendary kings was Romulus, the founder of Rome. Numa Pompilius was the second king, and he invented most of the Romans' religious ceremonies. Traditionally, the first Roman calendar is also attributed to King Numa. The third king, Tullus Hostilius, was known for his warmongering attitude. After him came Ancus Marcius, who founded Ostia as a seaport. Lucius Tarquinius Priscus, who is also known as "Tarquin the Elder," developed the Forum and the Circus Maximus, where the first Roman games took place. After him, Rome was ruled by Servius Tullius, who invented the Roman census to implement a tax system. The seventh and last king of Rome was Lucius Tarquinius Superbus, also known as "Tarquin the Proud." He was a tyrant, and his behavior toward the citizens of Rome led to a revolution that would start the republic.

Unfortunately, as mentioned above, the existence of these kings can't be confirmed. The later ruling families of Rome were known to make up their family history so they could claim family ties with the old rulers, which would give them legitimacy. The historians who described the deeds of these supposed kings were often hired by such families. Those who worked independently often misunderstood myths for reality and wrote fantastical stories that are hard to believe today. The mythical elements in the works of early historians occur quite often. For example, King Servius Tullius was conceived in a similar way as Romulus. In his story, a phallus emerged from the sacred fire and impregnated his mother. However, this is just an obvious example of mythical interference with history. We cannot be certain which parts of the stories might be truth or legend. As we saw, the archaeological evidence that Rome was a monarchy exists, but it doesn't explain to what extent. What were his duties, and what was the throne inheritance system like?

It is hard to establish the political system that the early Roman kings practiced. History was written half a millennium later, and Livy and his contemporary historians applied the modern political system to the past. They believed the Roman Kingdom had institutions such as the Senate, or an assembly of the people. But these were part of the city's political life from the republic and imperial eras. According to Roman historians, succession wasn't hereditary, but the kings were chosen by the people and ratified by the Senate. Once a king died, there was an interregnum period when a "between king" was chosen. Each of the seven legendary kings had a remarkably long reign of approximately thirty-five years. Such long reigns are impossible to believe, which leads scholars to believe the monarchy period was much shorter than the Roman historians have led us to believe or that there were more than seven kings, but they remain obscured by history.

If Rome was anything like other ancient settlements of Italy, it was a very small city at the beginning, numbering around a few thousand citizens. Kingship on this scale must have been very different from what was assumed by the first Roman historians. The institutions described in their work wouldn't matter on such a small scale, and therefore, it is believed that the king was the ultimate ruler. If the Senate existed, its function was probably reduced to the king's council, and they had no executive power. The legend of Romulus claims that the first king founded the Senate by choosing 300 men to be his councilors. However, this number might be exaggerated. It is more logical that it would have been reduced to three representatives of the tribes who inhabited early Rome: the Latins, Sabines, and the Etruscans.

The seven legendary kings of Rome are just an extension of the foundation myth. They were the successors of Romulus, and they continued to build the city and its institutions. But if one is to believe the old historians, the first Romans could have been anyone. Their ethnicity didn't matter as long as they gained citizenship in one way or another. Even the kings were not strictly Latin. Numa was believed to be Sabine, while Tarquinius Priscus was Etruscan. Servius Tullius was, by some accounts, a son of a slave, which proves that citizens of Rome could rise from the lowest rungs of society and become kings.

According to the early historians, the founder of the Roman religion was Numa Pompilius, but he wasn't a holy figure himself as Moses or Buddha. Numa was just a mortal who established religious rituals that would secure the prosperity of the city and its people. Roman religion is quite different from what we understand as religion today. They didn't believe in gods, but they knew that gods existed. They had no doctrine or a holy book that would connect morality with deities. In fact, Roman religion never even considered morality or personal salvation. The important part of the religion were the rituals, which were supposed to keep the relationship between the gods and the city strong. It always included some kind of sacrifice, often animals. The ritual itself was supposed to please the gods—not the belief in them or prayers dedicated to them. So, what was Numa's role in establishing the religion? He founded different groups of priests, whose job was to perform or overlook the rituals to make sure they were done properly. He also devised a calendar of twelve months, which gave the framework on which holy days and festivals could be established.

While Numa's priority was religion, Servius Tullius secured the prosperity of Rome through his political reforms. The first census of Rome was attributed to him, in which he classified citizens by their wealth. He also divided the Roman citizens into two major institutions: the Roman army and the voting body. He organized the army into 193 "centuries" based on the type of military equipment they wielded. Of course, the military equipment a soldier wielded depended on his wealth. According to the census, at the top of the army were the eight richest men, who had full bronze armor. Below them were four more classes, progressively wearing lighter and lighter armor. The fifth class, consisting of thirty centuries, were men who fought with only slings and stones. Above the fifth class were the elite cavalry, as well as military engineers and musicians. The voting body was very similar to the military, but instead of equipment, the richest citizens had the most voting power. The few richest citizens could outvote a mob of commoners. But the system was much more complicated than it seems. It involved different ways of calculating one's riches and evaluating the worth of their estates, houses, family members, and so on.

Some of the legendary Roman kings were given Etruscan ethnicity, and for a long time, scholars were confused by this. Tarquinius Priscus came to Rome because he was in search of prosperity. His father was Greek, and he believed that he would be treated as a foreigner in Etruria. Upon arriving in Rome, he rose to be its king. His story probably represents the migration of the Etruscans southward. However, some speculate this migration turned into a conquest during the reign of the next two kings, Servius Tullius and Tarquinius Superbus. There is no archaeological evidence to support the idea of military conquest. Perhaps the conflict did not occur, but the Etruscans did rule Rome for some time, which leads us to believe that Rome was in Etruscan possession during this period. There is plenty of evidence that Etruscan culture influenced Rome; even texts in the Etruscan language were found in the ruins of the city. But still, there is nothing to suggest a major conflict or military takeover.

Tyranny, Rape, and Freedom

The Roman monarchy fell somewhere in the 6th century, although the exact date cannot be pinpointed. According to the early Roman historians, the fall of the last Roman king occurred in 509, but this date is as mythological as the story that envelops it. Following the Greek tradition, Romans often connected a sexual assault with the end of one regnal period and the beginning of another. The story of Rome's foundation started with the rape of the Sabine women. Romulus's reign started with sexual aggression— why wouldn't the monarchy he founded end with one? It is perhaps the most famous of all: the rape of Lucretia. This time, the perpetrator wasn't a king but one of his sons. However mythical this story might be, it marks a turning point for the political system of Rome. Again, Livy is the historian who colorfully wrote the story of Lucretia's rape for future generations.

A group of young Romans were bored and needed to pass the time while besieging the nearby city of Ardea. One evening, they got drunk and started arguing whose wife was better. To end the argument, Lucius Tarquinius Collatinus suggested they all go home and inspect the women to determine which one was the best. The young men returned to Rome, which was only a few miles away, and found their wives partying in their absence. Only Lucretia was acting as a proper Roman wife, working the loom surrounded by her maids. She offered a meal to her husband, Lucius Tarquinius Collatinus, and his friends. But suddenly, Sextus Tarquinius desired Lucretia, and later on, he came to her demanding sex. He threatened to kill her, but she was unmoved by this. Then, Sextus threatened he would disgrace her by killing a slave next to her, so it would seem as if she had a relationship with a lowborn. Afraid of dishonor, Lucretia succumbed and gave herself to her husband's friend. Unable to live in peace, she sent for her husband and father, and once she told them of her disgrace, she killed herself.

To the Romans, the story of Lucretia served as an example of a perfect Roman wife, one who would gladly sacrifice her life to save the honor of the family. She is a perfect example of what the relationship between a husband and wife should be in ancient Rome. But strangely enough, Lucretia's story served as an excuse to get rid of the monarchs of the time. One of her husband's friends, Lucius Junius Brutus, took the dagger with which the heroine killed herself and swore he would end the monarchy. After all, the violence upon this perfect Roman wife was committed by none other than the king's son. Junius Brutus won the support of both the people and the army, and together, they expelled Sextus Tarquinius from Rome along with his father, Tarquinius Superbus.

But the royal family didn't leave the city without putting up a fight. Tarquinius Superbus attempted a counter-revolution, but he failed. Then he joined forces with King Lars Porsenna of Clusium. However, the newly liberated citizens found strength in their freedom and fought heroically, defeating the enemy. Scholars question if the monarchy ended right then and there. Even some of the ancient historians, such as Pliny the Elder, believed that Tarquinius Superbus perished during the conflict, but his ally, Etruscan King Lars Porsenna, conquered Rome and ruled it for some time.

The gods, Castor and Pollux, were supposedly seen fighting on the side of the Roman citizens, and a temple dedicated to them was erected in the Forum at the place where they supposedly watered their horses. This temple was rebuilt on many occasions, but it still stands, to this day, as one of the earliest symbols of Roman freedom. Today, it is a famous landmark of Rome's history and a monument to the fall of the monarchy.

With the end of the monarchy, the title *Rex* (king) became a term of loathing in Roman politics. Even though it was the kings who founded and organized the city-state, they were no longer wanted or welcomed in Rome. Despite this, the city never had a problem admitting its origin or the fact that it used to be a monarchy. People never tried to rewrite history; they simply remembered it in the form of stories that turned into legends and myths. Many politicians were accused of striving to become a monarch, and such an accusation was dangerous, as it could end one's political career. The people's hatred toward royalty is best displayed through the continuation of Lucretia's myth. Her husband was tied to the monarch's family, even though it is unclear what his relationship was with the king. But Lucius Tarquinius Collatinus was a Tarquinius, and as such, he had to leave Rome. It wasn't enough that he lost his wife due to the monarchy; his name also became a curse to him, and he was exiled.

Rome's hatred for kings extended even outside the city. Whenever there was a war, the preferred enemy was a king, who was always portrayed as the embodiment of evil and oppression. It was a special occasion when a triumph parade was organized with a tied-up foreign king, who was mocked, often beaten, and eventually executed for simply being a king. The people's attitude toward the kingship sped up the process of Rome gaining freedom and starting a republic, which occurred at the end of the 6th century BCE. The people of Rome chose the name "republic" because of its core meaning, "public affairs" (res publica). The city was now the property of all of its people, not just the monarch.

Chapter 3 – The Roman Republic

Traditionally, the date chosen to represent the birth of the Roman Republic is 509 BCE. In the same year, it is believed King Tarquinius was exiled to Etruria, and Rome entered a new age. Romans later believed that Rome acquired its cityscape during the first year of the republic. Many famous buildings, such as the Temple of Jupiter, were built by previous kings, but they were attributed to the republic instead. In Roman minds, nothing should be associated with the monarchy anymore; all that was good in the city must have had its origin in freedom, in the republic.

With the new freedom came the new political system. Instead of a king, two consuls were chosen to run the realm's affairs. Each of them had the power to veto the other one. This way, they could keep each other in check, and none of them was able to grasp too much power. The first consuls of Rome are unknown, but legend has it that it was none other than Brutus and Lucretia's husband, Collatinus. The consuls did not only preside over the city's senate and decide internal politics, but they were also the war leaders. Consuls were never really the antithesis of a king. They continued to have all the power of the monarch, but since they were split in two, it ensured no tyranny could emerge.

However, there were differences between the kings and consuls. While consuls were elected by the Senate, just like kings, they held that position for only one year. This means they had no time to gather enough power to rise to the position of a monarch. They also didn't have enough time to work solely on personal interests and were forced to make decisions that would benefit the city as a whole. The Romans started naming the years after the consuls who presided at the time. They didn't have the modern standard of calculating the time as we do. For them, the year 63 BCE would mean nothing. Instead, they would say the wine they are drinking is from the year of "Marcus Tullius Cicero and Gaius Antonius Hybrida" because they presided over that specific year. The Roman Forum had a list of all the consuls who were elected since the beginning of the republic. Alongside it was a list of generals who were granted triumphal entrance into the city due to a famous victory in war. Ancient historians used this list as a tool to pinpoint the end of the monarchy.

The Roman Republic became so much more than a political system. It became a symbol of freedom, time, the city's landscape, and culture. The republic became the identity of Rome's citizens, for which they were proud, just as the Greeks of Athens were proud of their democracy. And maybe it is not accidental that both Rome and Athens liberated themselves from their tyrants at the same time, at the end of 6th century BCE (509 and 508 BCE, respectively). While Greece gave birth to democracy, Rome created its republic.

Two Centuries of Change

To ancient Romans, the transition from a monarchy to a republic was smooth and perfect. The story says that the first consuls were chosen immediately, and the new political system was completely set in place during the first year of the republic. However, archaeological excavations tell a different story. It seems the transition was very gradual and took decades, maybe even a century or more, to establish the republic and its principles. Many titles were given to the heads of political power, and they predate the consuls. For example, "Chief Predator" and "Dictator" were titles that originated in the early republic, but these titles are not something we would connect with freedom and equal rule today. Instead, they speak of some form of hierarchy in the early republic. But we are unable to pinpoint exactly when the true Roman Republic emerged and when the Romans chose their first consuls. Even the famous Livy admits that it is impossible to sort the chronology of the early Roman consuls without mistakes. Today, scholars believe that some of the consuls from the Forum's list were made up to fill the gaps and serve the purpose of confirming the mythological first consuls Brutus and Collatinus.

The first found inscription that mentions a consul is dated to the 3rd century BCE, two centuries after the Roman stories claim the republic started. This consul was Lucius Cornelius Scipio Barbatus, and he was a consul at around 298 BCE, a time that was very different from when the republic began. In the 3rd century BCE, Rome numbered anywhere between 60,000 and 90,000 citizens. For comparison, at the same time, Athens had around 40,000 citizens. Rome also had control of the territory around the city, and at this point, it spread from coast to coast. Roughly half a million people lived outside the city but were under Rome's jurisdiction. In addition, the city had a series of agreements and treaties with neighboring cities, and through conquest, it constantly added more people under Rome's rule. It is believed that even during the Roman Empire, Rome never again had so many people under its direct control.

By this time, Rome had developed its recognizable political system and hierarchy. Under the two consuls, there was a series of state officials occupying different positions. The highest ranks, which were just below the consuls, were the praetors and quaestors, collectively called the magistrates. They either managed a specific geographical region (a province) or wielded a certain constitutional power. They were responsible for defining sentences for crimes, and they also had to look for omens that would decide the fate of the city. They were elected by the people of Rome. The magistrate office was also annual, and once it expired, the same person could only be elected after ten years had passed since he first served.

After a magistrate served, he would automatically become a member of the Roman Senate. During the republic, the Senate was the same as during the monarchy. Its main purpose was to advise consuls and magistrates, usually on the matters of foreign politics. Senators were not elected but rather appointed by the consuls. Their task was to advise and issue various decrees after a decision had been made and approved by the consuls. But the Senate also had the most power over the everyday life of Rome. Because they were in direct control of the administration, foreign policy, and money, they could influence all spheres of life. The office for senator was for life, unlike the office for consul or magistrate. But because there were so many of them, senators weren't able to grasp too much power and turn into tyrants.

The Constitution of the Roman Republic stated the people had the ultimate power. And this is true to some extent. It was the people who formed the legislative assembly, which consisted t of all the free Roman citizens, and they would elect the consuls and magistrates. This assembly also had the power to carry out Roman law, be it a declaration of war or a punishment of a criminal. They had no representatives. Each citizen was a part of the legislative assembly as long as he was a free adult citizen; women were not allowed to be on the assembly. There were two assemblies, and each had power over different political aspects. While the Comitia Centuriata ("Centuriate Assembly") dealt with the military issues and the election of censors, the Comitia Tributa ("Tribal Assembly") dealt with the election of quaestors and the military tribune. They also dealt with most of the Roman laws. The Comitia Tributa was not based on ethnicity but on geographical regions.

Aside from the political changes that occurred during the Roman Republic, this period also saw the first issuing of coinage and the abrupt development of the city's infrastructure. The first aqueduct was constructed in 312 BCE. It was an extraordinary system that brought water from the nearby hills directly into the city. But it wasn't as glamorous as today's aqueducts, as they were created on a much smaller scale and ran underground. The same person who constructed the first aqueduct, Appius Claudius Caecus, constructed the first major Roman road, the Via Appia. This road was also constructed in 312 BCE, and it led straight from Rome to Capua. This road was mainly used for communication and the military, but travelers, merchants, and citizens used it for their private matters too. Even though it was just a gravel road for most of its life, the Via Appia became the symbol of Roman power because of its diverse use and the power to accommodate everyone.

At some point between 500 and 300 BCE, the Romans defined what it meant to be a Roman citizen. It wasn't just the citizenship policy that separated Rome from the other city-states of the Latin world and beyond. But it wasn't an easy road that led to the definition of Roman citizenship as we understand it now, or as the Romans themselves understood it back then. It consisted of a series of civil fights, mutinies, and another rape. In the end, the common people, the "plebeians," won their freedom and the right to be politically equal with the elite, the "patricians." In the past, only the patricians were truly free. They were the wealthy upper class of Rome who held all the political power in their hands. The plebeians were the working class, and they had very few rights. For 200 years, the plebeians instigated a series of fights and strikes, refusing even to serve the army. This fight gradually brought them more and more rights, and eventually, they were able to hold the political offices and even marry into the patrician class.

But the early Roman Republic didn't have only internal conflicts. The city spread its influence to surrounding areas through conquest. After decades of warfare with the Etruscan city of Veii, Rome won a decisive victory in 396 BCE. Soon, Rome was challenged by the invading Gauls and had to defend its newly conquered areas to the north. With the military demands came the need to reorganize the army and make it more efficient. At first, the Roman army copied the Etruscan one. It was due to the influence of their northern neighbor that the Romans introduced phalanx formations, which is of Greek origin. But it was the war against their southern neighbor, the Samnites, that inspired the change in the army's formation. Because the enemy lived in a hilly region, on the slopes of the Apennine Mountains, the area wasn't vast enough for a typical phalanx formation, so it had to be changed into a manipular formation. This change is attributed to a certain Marcus Furius Camillus, whom modern scholars believe was as mythological as Romulus himself. *Maniples* were composed of 120 men, and they were divided into three lines depending on the type of infantry they represented. The first lines were the *hastati*, who wore heavy bronze plate armor and wielded a shield, sword, and two throwing spears. The second line consisted of the *principes*, who were dressed in leather and mail armor and carried the same weapons as the first line. The third line was named *triarii*, and they also wore mail armor, but instead of wielding swords and shields, they were equipped with a light spear.

The Twelve Tables

According to tradition, in 494 BCE, a large group of the plebs (plebeians) left the city of Rome and occupied the Sacred Mount overlooking the city. They did this because they were oppressed by the patricians, who treated them almost as slaves, even though they officially enjoyed the free status of a citizen. The citizens who left Rome organized their own political system, known as the *Concilium Plebis* ("Plebian Council"), which was an alternative state with separate officials and an assembly of people. Back in Rome, life screeched to a halt. The plebs were the working force of the city, as they occupied the positions of bakers, artisans, farmers, potters, blacksmiths, and so on. The First Secession, as this event became known, led the Roman patricians to promise additional rights to the plebs.

The struggle for freedom and political rights continued over the decades, and with each threat of a new secession, Roman patricians would promise new rights to the common citizens. However, a promise was not the same as a law, and the plebs had to fight again to secure the law that would defend their rights. By 464 BCE, the laws concerning plebs were installed, but since they were not written, everyone had the right to interpret them as they wished. This was not good enough for the working class of Rome, and they demanded the laws and regulations be written down and available to the public at all times, or else a new succession would occur. In 454 BCE, the wealthy upper class had to abide by this, and they organized a group of ten men, known as the *Decemviri Legibus Scribundis*, who would go to Greece and study their laws so they could come up with a similar solution.

After the delegation returned from Athens, they gathered to draft a code of laws. The current consuls and the tribune of plebs abdicated and gave the imperium (right to rule) to the Decemviri for one year. In that year, 451 BCE, they came up with the ten "tables" of law, and the following year, two more were added. But when it was time for the second Decemviri to turn back the imperium, they refused. A new scandal shook Rome, and just as with the end of the monarchy, this attempted tyranny ended with rape.

The story goes that Appius Claudius Crassus, one of the Decemviri, had such a lust for power that he managed to bribe and intimidate people to get elected for the second time. He fell in love with a common girl named Verginia, the daughter of the famous centurion Lucius Verginius. Because she was a free Roman citizen and engaged to another man, Claudius came up with the plan to have one of his minions claim that the girl was his slave. This would allow him to rape Verginia without consequences. When Verginius tried to defend his daughter, he was not allowed to speak. To save her freedom and honor, he had no other choice but to kill Verginia. According to the tradition, it was this event that prompted the plebs to another secession. To end the crisis, Appius Claudius killed himself, and the plebs settled with the rest of the Decemviri. The Law of the Twelve Tables was publicly hanged in the Roman Forum.

Most of the laws written in the Twelve Tables concern domestic problems, and they mostly focus on family life, neighbors, private property, and death rituals. Abandoning deformed babies was a common practice during antiquity; modern scholars refer to it as "exposure," as babies were left to die alone in the wilderness. The early laws of Rome laid down the procedure on how one should properly abandon undesired offspring. Other procedures described in the Twelve Tables concern inheritance and funerals. Women were banned from harming themselves while mourning the dead, and the funeral fires were to be lit at a safe distance from the house. Most of the commoner's worries were about neighbors behaving badly, letting their animals destroy other people's property. They were worried about thieves, vandals, and even magic. People were punished if accused of bewitching crops, animals, or even other people.

The Twelve Tables were the foundation of the Roman law, and they introduced equality, justice, and punishment in the lives of Roman citizens, whether they were plebeians or patricians. From the primitive form of the Twelve Tables, the Romans continued to build their law system, perfecting it through the centuries. Some universities around the world still teach Roman law in their curriculums, as it is the basis of today's civil law for most of the countries in the Western world.

The Gallic Attack and the Roman Expansion

By 390 BCE, the Po Valley was inhabited by the Celts, who had migrated there. That year, they crossed the Apennines and attacked northern Etruria. From there, they continued their advance down the Tiber River Valley to the south, reaching the outskirts of Rome. The Romans hastily gathered an army, but they could not match the invaders. At the River Allia, they were defeated. Only a few days later, the Celts entered the city and sacked it. But the Gauls were not interested in conquest. They only wanted the riches, and they soon left Rome.

This episode of Roman history resonated throughout the world. It is still considered one of the most important events of Roman history. Even Greek writers from the 4th century BCE often mention the sacking of Rome in their works. The tradition often exaggerates the extent of the damage caused to the city. Some stories talk about a large number of lives being lost, but the written evidence suggests that people escaped the city just before the attack, meaning the casualties were minimal. Later on, the traditional stories talk about Rome being destroyed. However, there is no archaeological evidence that would suggest the city's destruction at any time during the 4th century. A layer of burnt ruins was found, but it was dated to the 6th century BCE; therefore, it is impossible to match the story of the Gallic attack.

Even if the city wasn't destroyed and the casualties were minimal, the event still had a profound impact on the further development of Rome and what it later became. The successful military campaigns and the expansion of Rome that followed in the years immediately after speaks about Rome's remarkable ability to recover. If the sacking of Rome didn't destroy the city, it was, for sure, a severe blow to the morale of its citizens. To lift spirits and to persuade the citizens of their unity, a quick victory was needed.

Rome recovered so quickly that some scholars believe the Gallic attack never really happened and that it was all a fabrication of propaganda writers of later centuries. This opinion is supported by the lack of archaeological evidence. However, the modern consensus is that the attack did happen, but it was greatly exaggerated by later writers who tried to lift the scale of the event and present the Romans as great victors in the end. To support this, an analysis of the works of historians who touched on the theme is necessary. Livy was the first to give an elaborate account of the battle, and he includes an episode where a famous Roman military commander in exile, Marcus Furius Camillus, saved the city by ambushing and massacring the Gauls in their sleep. This episode of Camillus is not mentioned in any other account. The belief is that the great Roman military commander is a fabrication that served the purpose of propaganda. Other older historians mention that the Gauls were defeated on their way back from Rome once they reached Caere, an Etruscan city that allied itself with Rome during the conflict with Veii.

The expansion of Rome began before the Gallic attack, and it was merely interrupted by the raid. Since the beginning of the Roman Republic, Rome was at war with Etruria, and in 396, Veii was conquered. Soon, the cities of Tarquinii, Aequi, and Volsci fell, and the Romans started founding the Latin colonies in Etruria. The first colonies were Sutrium (Sutri) and Nepet (modern-day Nepi) in the south, which were probably founded around 383 BCE. From the beginning of the expansion until the early 4th century, Rome expanded its territory around 75 percent. The ability to do so proves that Rome was very powerful and that the Gallic raid did not manage to stop the momentum of the Roman expansion. The capture of Veii brought most of the territorial expansion to Rome, and its annexation in 396 meant that Rome was now enriched by another new 700 square kilometers. Before 495, Rome's territory was around 900 square kilometers, and in 396, it was 1,582 square kilometers. It should be noted that not all this territory was due to the conquest of Veii. The people of these conquered regions were given Roman citizenship, creating four new tribes: the Stellatina, Arniensis, Sabatina, and Tromentina.

Caere was the first known ally of Rome, and it seems the cities had a unique friendship, which was confirmed by a treaty that guaranteed a restricted form of citizenship known as *civitas sine suffragio* (citizenship without suffrage). This meant that if the citizens of Caere found themselves in Rome, they would all have the privileges of Roman citizens but not their obligations. The same would be with a Roman who entered Caere. The alliance was made because Caere was a powerful Etruscan city, and it wouldn't allow Rome to annex it. Instead, Rome offered this unique treaty, and Caere showed its gratitude during the conquest of Veii and during the Gallic attack when it took in the refugees and the Roman Vestal priestesses.

Rome made the same treaty with Massilia after the invasion by the Gauls. Tradition tells that this city helped Rome gather a ransom to pay the Gauls to leave the city. In gratitude, Massilia's citizens were welcomed in Rome just as the Caereans. With two strong allies, it is no wonder Rome made a quick recovery after the Gallic attacks and was able to resume its expansion policy. By the 360s, Rome was strong enough to start the gradual but successful conquest of all of Italy.

In 362, the conquest policy of Rome was renewed with an attack on the Hernici, a Latin tribe. This tribe used to be one of the smaller allies of Rome before the Gallic attack, but it abandoned the treaty after seeing the great Rome being defeated by the Celtic tribes. By 358, Rome defeated the Hernici, and the alliance between the two peoples was renewed. One of the clauses of the new treaty was that the Hernici had to give up a part of their territory so it could be settled by Roman citizens. After taking the territory of the Trerus Valley, Rome created two new tribes, the Pomptina and the Publilia, which were now under the jurisdiction of the city-state.

Latium was again threatened by the Gauls when the Romans and the Hernici were allying. At the same time, from 361 until 354, Rome was at war with the Tiburtines, who were joined by the Gauls. By the end of the war, another tribe joined the Tiburtines and the Gauls: the Praeneste. However, Rome was able to defeat this alliance and subdue them with a treaty. In 353, the previously allied Caere joined forces with Tarquinia against Rome. The outcome of this war was a new truce between the cities, which lasted for the next 100 years.

In 349, the expansion policy of Rome was interrupted once more by a Gallic attack, but they were easily defeated. Rome made peace with this Celtic tribe, and it was left undisturbed for the next thirty years. It is unclear whether these periodic attacks by the Gauls were meant to be full-scale invasions or only occasional raids. Whatever happened, it is clear that Rome learned how to deal with these attacks, but that doesn't mean Rome didn't suffer during these raids. They were so bloody and savage that the mention of Gauls would cause a panic in the city. The last three invasions of the Gauls, in 228, 216, and 114, brought so much panic that the Romans started human sacrifices to please the gods and avoid the destruction of the city.

However, the Roman army continued to grow and improve. The external policy of the city-state didn't change. If anything, Rome became even more ambitious, as it started conquering its neighbors one by one. In 357, they raided Privernum, and in 345, they targeted Aurunci and Sora. But the years between 343 and 290 were largely dominated by three wars against the Samnites, a group of people who occupied the territory south of Rome. The Samnites were a coalition of Oscan-speaking tribes: the Caraceni, Hirpini, Caudini, Frentani, and Pentri. These tribes allied against Rome. During the first conflict, Rome spread its influence to the city-state of Capua, with which it started an alliance. From 340 until 349, Rome continued to conquer southward, and it annexed many Latin cities, spreading its dominion. But the Roman conquest policy only further angered the Samnites, who answered by instigating another war in 326. This time, Rome was defeated, and it was forced to accept a truce that favored the Samnite tribes. We already learned that Rome did not take a defeat lightly, and a series of victories followed according to the tradition. However, modern scholars believe these victories were fabrications that served the propaganda of the time. Rome was defeated by the Samnites, and its expansion was halted for the time being.

The hostilities were soon renewed in 317 BCE for unknown reasons. Rome was defeated in the initial battle, but it started winning gradually. By 304, Roman captured a major Samnite city, Bovianum, forcing its enemy to plead for peace. But the Samnites never forgave Rome for its effort to impose its dominance over their tribal territories. Later, some of them would join Hannibal Barca in the Punic Wars against Rome. The Samnites would also take part in the civil wars that would destroy the Roman Republic, but it would cease to exist as a separate ethnicity during the Roman Empire, as they would be completely integrated into Roman society.

The Punic Wars

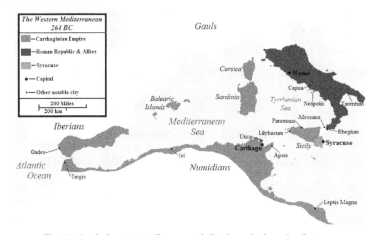

Territories belonging to Rome and Carthage before the first war
Jon Platek, CC BY-SA 3.0 <https://creativecommons.org/licenses/by-sa/3.0>, via Wikimedia Commons https://commons.wikimedia.org/wiki/File:First_Punic_War_264_BC.png

Hannibal ante portas. This expression was attributed to Marcus Tullius Cicero, and it was used to scare ancient Roman children who behaved badly. Hannibal Barca was the nemesis of the Romans during the Second Punic War (218-201), and propaganda spread that the evil Carthaginian general would take the children of the city. But this expression was first used to describe a great imminent danger and the people who do nothing to avoid it. "Hannibal is at the gates" is the meaning of this old Latin expression, and it marks the age of the great wars between Rome and Carthage, which wrestled for the dominion over the Mediterranean world.

The history of the Punic Wars starts before Hannibal crossed the Alps and threatened the city itself. It starts with an alliance between the two great cities. The Roman Republic's expansion to the south brought them in conflict with the Greek colony Tarentum. In response to Roman aggression, this colony asked King Pyrrhus of Epirus for help. This adventurous king came with an army and defeated the Romans in two separate battles, stopping their advance. But another Greek colony had a similar problem. Sicily was suffering attacks by Carthage, a city in Africa (in today's Tunisia), which had been founded by Phoenician merchants. Pyrrhus responded to the Sicilian pleas for help, but it only resulted in an alliance between Rome and Carthage in 279 BCE against their common enemy. This alliance was very strange. Even though both sides promised to send military aid upon the request of the other, Carthage never asked for Rome's involvement while fighting against the Greek king. As a result, it lost all of its possessions in Sicily.

King Pyrrhus set sail to Italy to face the Romans once again in 275 BCE, but on his way across the Strait of Messina, he was attacked by Carthaginian mercenaries. The Carthaginians won the naval battle, but the Greek king managed to save the majority of his army and approach Rome, which was, at the time, fighting with the Samnites. The two armies clashed in the Battle of Beneventum, where the Romans managed to win by injuring a young elephant. Being only a youngster, the elephant ran away in search of his mother, causing a commotion among all the Greek elephants. This was the first time Italy ever saw this animal, and the Romans managed to capture eight of them and learned how to use them in their future wars. The commotion among the elephants caused panic in the ranks of Pyrrhus's army, and the Romans easily turned the battle in their favor.

After the defeat, Pyrrhus set sail for Greece, leaving Sicily and the other Greek colonies at the mercy of the two Mediterranean powers. Rome was now free to continue its conquest southward, and the first to suffer was again the city of Tarentum. But this time, the Greek colony asked Carthage for help, and in 272 BCE, the African city broke its alliance with Rome. This was the first conflict between Rome and Carthage, but the First Punic War would occur almost a decade later. After the victory at Tarentum, Rome spent the next eight years spreading its influence over the southern Italian ports to dominate the eastern Mediterranean, a territory in which Carthage invested much interest. It was the trade interest of these two cities that instigated the First Punic War in 264 BCE, as Rome wanted to conquer Sicily. Their first objective was the city of Messana (today's Messina), where Carthage already had a garrison.

The First Punic War started when a Roman consul, Appius Claudius Caudex, crossed the Strait of Messina with around 20,000 men to capture Messana. There, he met a symbolic resistance of the superior Punic navy, but the Carthaginian garrison stationed in the city fled. Appius Claudius managed to capture one of the Punic ships, which would later be copied and improved to create the great Roman navy. To make it clear, Punic refers to Carthage. Romans called the citizens of Carthage *Poeni,* and the modern transformation of that word gave us the name for the series of conflicts.

The Carthage commander in Sicily was Hanno. He entered an alliance with Hiero II of Syracuse to relieve the city of Messana from the Romans. However, the outcome of the battle is unknown. Both Hiero II and Appius Claudius retreated, and history doesn't remember if the Romans won or were beaten. The following year saw the two Roman consuls arriving in Sicily, accompanied by 40,000 men. The Sicilian cities sided with the Romans after seeing their power. Once they reached Syracuse, Hiero had to sue for peace. But Carthage wasn't dormant during these times. It gathered mercenaries from Spain, Gaul, and Liguria and stationed them at Agrigentum on the southwest shore of Sicily. In 262, the battle between Carthage and Rome took place in this city, which Rome won. The commander of the Carthaginian army, Hannibal (not to be confused with the more famous Hannibal Barca), sent for help.

Back in Africa, Carthage managed to gather a great army and send it to Sicily under the command of Hanno. However, they were unable to defeat the Romans, and they took the battle to the sea, where they hoped they had the advantage. Although Carthage had the greater naval force and superior ships, the Romans developed a method of using boarding ramps, which allowed them to transfer their soldiers onto the Punic ships to fight in melee combat. Carthage lost the naval battle, but the Romans were unable to remove them from the western part of Sicily. Instead, they decided to invade Africa.

A new Roman consul was elected in 256. His name was Marcus Atilius Regulus, and he took a very large force to Africa. They landed near Aspis, and they raided its surroundings. Carthage achieved its first victory in 255 BCE when they raised an army under the command of Xanthippus, a Spartan mercenary. At the Bagradas River, he annihilated the Roman army but took 500 prisoners, among which was Consul Regulus.

In 254, the First Punic War returned to Sicily, where the Romans took the city of Panormus (modern-day Palermo). This was enough to temporarily stop the conflict, and Carthage took its time to reorganize its army. No new battles occurred until 251/250 BCE when Punic leader Hasdrubal tried to retake Panormus. Unfortunately, he was defeated by the Roman consul Caecilius Metellus. The war dragged on for a few more years, in which naval battles were very dominant. Rome realized the strength of Carthage lay in their ships, so they quickly built a stronger and larger fleet. The final naval battle occurred in 241 BCE near the Aegates Islands. The Carthaginian fleet was defeated, and they were forced to sue for peace. The Treaty of Lutatius concluded the twenty-three-year-long First Punic War. Carthage promised they would leave Sicily and pay a war indemnity to Rome.

The First Punic War cost Carthage much more than just Sicily. Carthage was unable to pay its mercenaries for their services, which led to a rebellion that took two years to subdue. At first, Rome didn't want to take advantage of the unrest in their enemy's territory, but toward the end of the rebellion, Rome seized the opportunity to take Corsica and Sardinia from Carthage, breaking the Treaty of Lutatius. However, torn by conflict with Rome and the rebellion of the mercenaries, Carthage was unable to respond. Instead, an internal change was about to happen. A new political party, led by Hamilcar Barca, came to power. He was determined to return the previous dominance over the Mediterranean to Carthage. To achieve this, he needed a new base of power, and he chose Spain.

In 237, he set sail and spent the next nine years campaigning in Spain. He died there in 229, but his young sons, Hannibal and Hasdrubal, managed to escape the wrath of the local Spanish tribe leader. The brothers were too young to inherit their father's command, and it was, at first, given to their brother-in-law, Hasdrubal the Elder, also called Hasdrubal the Fair. He continued Hamilcar's ambitions in Spain and consolidated Carthaginian control in the Iberian Peninsula but was soon killed by the rebels. The Punic army stationed in Spain chose Hannibal as their leader, and the campaign against the Spanish tribes continued uninterrupted.

Rome had interests in Spain too, and a deal was made with Carthage that the boundary between the two rivals would be the Ebro River. Carthage was allowed to operate south of the river, while the north belonged to Rome. The only exception was the town of Saguntum, which was to stay neutral. Hannibal, who was only twenty-six at the time, attacked the neutral town, provoking the Romans in 219 BCE. After several months of siege, Saguntum fell, and Hannibal executed most of its citizens. This enraged Rome to the point where a new war was declared.

Carthage needed to keep the war away from its center base in Africa, where its main agricultural lands were. This would ensure that the city and its surrounding areas would have uninterrupted access to food during the war. Rome planned to invade Africa, but Carthage was faster, as its government quickly sent Hannibal to bring the war to Rome's gates. But to do this, the Punic commander had to cross the Alps. He turned to the Gauls for help, but his diplomacy wasn't as successful as he hoped. While some Gauls agreed to join him, most of the Celtic tribes refused to help and instead opposed his crossing. In fact, during the fifteen days it took Hannibal to cross, Hannibal's troops were constantly under Gallic attacks. He began the endeavor with 50,000 infantry, 9,000 cavalry, and 37 elephants. The harsh environment of the mountains took many lives, as did the Gauls. When Hannibal crossed the Alps, he was left with only 20,000 infantry and 6,000 cavalry. All the elephants survived the passage.

In response to Hannibal, Rome appointed Publius Cornelius Scipio to lead the army. The first conflict between the two commanders occurred at the Ticinus River in 218 BCE. The Carthaginians won this battle easily. Scipio was even wounded, but he managed to flee with the help of his son, who would soon be known as Scipio "Africanus," the greatest enemy of Hannibal Barca.

The Roman consul, Tiberius Sempronius Longus, marched to the north, where he joined forces with Scipio. Together, they fought Hannibal at the Trebia River. Hannibal took advantage of the bad weather and the battlefield's terrain to defeat the Romans. Even though the Carthaginians didn't lose many people, they were left with only one surviving elephant.

Winter was fast approaching, and Hannibal decided to spend it at Placentia (today's Piacenza in the Emilia-Romagna region). This gave Rome time to gather a new army. However, Hannibal soon crossed the Apennines, not allowing the two Roman consuls to join their armies. Instead, he inflicted a defeat first on Consul Gaius Flaminius at Lake Trasimene and then moved quickly to meet the other consul, Gnaeus Servilius Geminus, at Ariminum (Rimini). After defeating both Roman forces, Hannibal was free to move on Rome. The panic caused by the Carthaginian victories in Italy was so great that the Romans decided to elect a dictator. A dictator was only chosen in times of great need. This title was only given to one person, who would replace the two consuls and had all the power to make the decisions and move the armies how he saw fit. The chosen dictator was Fabius Maximus, who ordered people from the countryside to move behind the walls of the cities. He also destroyed all the bridges over the Tiber River to stop Hannibal from approaching the city, and he laid waste to the fields around Rome to deprive the Carthaginians access to resources.

But Hannibal had no intention of marching directly on Rome. Instead, he crossed the Apennines again and went to Picenum (on the northern coast of the Adriatic Sea). Rome chose not to send its full army after the Carthaginians. Instead, Fabius ordered constant harassment of the Punic army, although he prohibited an open battle. Winter was approaching again, and Hannibal chose to spend it in Apulia, located in southern Italy. The dictator did not completely deal with the Punic invasion, but he managed to discourage Hannibal from attacking Rome itself. In 216 BCE, two new consuls were elected: Marcus Terentius Varro and Lucius Aemilius Paullus. Together, they decided to engage Hannibal in a decisive battle and end the open threat to Rome. They gathered the largest army possible, which numbered over 86,000 souls. They confronted the much-weaker Hannibal, who only had around 50,000 men. At the Battle of Cannae, which took place on August 2nd, 216 BCE, Hannibal was victorious in inflicting the greatest defeat Rome would ever experience throughout history.

The conflict between Carthage and Rome occurred in Spain too. In 218 BCE, the Romans defeated the Punic army, which was led by Hannibal's nephew, Hanno, at Cisa. Publius Cornelius Scipio joined the Spanish efforts in 216, but he was unable to retake Saguntum. In 215, Scipio fought against Hannibal's brother, Hasdrubal Barca, and was victorious, but he didn't believe he had enough momentum to push southward. Scipio spent the next two years gathering forces and consolidating Roman power north of the River Ebro. In 212 BCE, he finally took over Saguntum. The next year, he went on the offensive against the Carthaginian forces. However, Scipio decided to divide his forces, which was a fatal mistake. The Carthaginians easily defeated and even killed him.

Young Publius Cornelius Scipio arrived in Spain in 210 BCE, leading a large force. As if to avenge the death of his father, young Scipio captured the main power hub of the Carthaginians in Spain, which he renamed Nova Carthago ("New Carthage"). In 208, he defeated Hasdrubal Barca, and the next year, he defeated Hannibal's youngest brother, Mago Barca. By 206, Scipio brought the entire Iberian Peninsula under Roman dominion, crushing the Carthaginian resistance. Since the conflict in Spain ended, Scipio turned his mind toward Africa.

In Italy, Hannibal decided to march to Rome in 211 BCE. However, he hesitated. It seems he didn't want to confront Rome directly, but since the Romans easily reconquered some of the previously captured cities and towns, Hannibal had no other choice.

But Hannibal seemed to have lost his military focus. As soon as he saw the Roman defenses, filled with fresh recruits, he turned back and decided not to engage in any battle. Instead, he wintered in Apulia. The years of warfare seemed to exhaust both armies, and for the next two years, many inconclusive battles occurred, with neither side achieving anything. In 208 BCE, Hasdrubal decided to join his brother in Italy, and he took his army of approximately 20,000 men to the south. Hannibal rushed to the north of Italy to meet him, but he arrived too late. Hasdrubal's forces had already engaged the Romans led by Gaius Claudius Nero and were crushed. Hasdrubal was killed, and Nero sent his head to Hannibal. The Carthaginian commander was devastated by his brother's death, and no major conflict occurred in Italy throughout 206 BCE.

In the spring of 204, Scipio launched his forces to Africa, setting up camp near Utica. Meanwhile, the Romans allied with King Masinissa of Numidia, and they moved their cavalry forces inland. Their first victory was against Hannibal's nephew Hanno, near Salaeca. Carthage sent Hasdrubal Gisco to meet Scipio, and they agreed to stop the conflict until the spring. The opposing armies set up their winter camps opposing each other. Scipio was the first to attack as soon as spring came, burning the Punic camp down. Hasdrubal fled, but Scipio couldn't pursue him because of the political troubles back in Rome. Despite these internal problems, he didn't leave Africa.

Hannibal was recalled to Carthage in 203 BCE, where the conflict continued. The two commanders first confronted each other at the decisive Battle of Zama in 202. Even though the forces were fairly even, Roman discipline resulted in fewer losses compared to the Carthaginians, who mostly employed various mercenaries. Hannibal lost more than 25,000 men, and Scipio only lost around 5,000 Romans. This victory brought Scipio the title "Africanus," and the Carthaginians had to sue for peace. The treaty that signaled the end of the Second Punic War destroyed Carthage as a military and trade power in the Mediterranean. One of the treaty's clauses stated that Carthage would not engage in any military conflict without Rome's approval. The Numidians soon intruded on Carthaginian territory. When the Carthaginians tried to defend themselves, they achieved nothing except to give Rome an excuse to start the Third Punic War.

Numidia continued to be ruled by Rome's ally, Masinissa, who annexed some of Carthage's territories. In response, Carthage sent an army to regain that territory, but Rome saw their efforts as a direct attack on their Numidian ally. Already weakened, Carthage realized Rome was about to attack, and they quickly assembled defenses. The first Roman force came from Sicily and landed on African soil in Utica. The initial conflict of the Third Punic War occurred in the summer of 149 BCE, with the Romans directly attacking the city of Carthage. However, they were unable to take the city, so instead, they began an extended siege. The Romans did not achieve much until 148 BCE. A new consul was elected, Scipio Aemilianus, who came directly to Africa. Due to his genius engineering and building of moles (stone walls that separate bodies of water), he managed to cut Carthage off from its main supply lines, both on land and at sea. The siege lasted until 146, which was when the Roman army managed to gain a foothold near the city's harbor. This was enough to convince the Carthaginians, who were hiding in Byrsa (the city's citadel), to surrender. Unfortunately, the Romans decided to sack and burn the city for six days before accepting their surrender. They killed so many citizens that some scholars regard it as the first genocide committed in history. The last building to be burned was the Temple of Eshmun, but it was actually burned by the Carthaginian citizens, as they saw no hope. They chose to die in the flames rather than by the Romans' swords. Among them were even the wife and children of commander Hasdrubal (a different Hasdrubal than before).

Legend has it that Scipio Africanus ordered the destruction of Carthage, whose territory he plowed and covered in salt. This was a ritualistic practice that was supposed to curse the site so the city would never be rebuilt and reinhabited. But it seems this legend is of much older date, as the practice only existed in the Middle East. However, it became a common motif in medieval literature. Carthage was destroyed, but it was later rebuilt by Julius Caesar. Its territories were annexed and converted into a Roman province with its capital as Utica, which had remained loyal to Rome.

Chapter 4 – Social Wars and the End of the Roman Republic

The Mediterranean world was opened up to Rome with the end of the Punic Wars and its expansion to Corsica and Sardinia. The 2nd century BCE saw the influx of Greek people, culture, and customs into Italy. Rome found itself under this new Greek influence. Before that, the only contact the two countries had was through the few colonies Greece had in Italy, but these were not enough to majorly impact Rome. Now, it was a different story.

The first athletic games were organized by Scipio Africanus's brother in 186, and they were modeled on the Greek ones. At the end of the 3rd century, Greek drama and epic poems were introduced as well. By the middle of the 2nd century BCE, a Roman citizen with a higher social status was well acquainted with the Greek way of life. However, this foreign way of life threatened traditional Roman values, and many citizens were aware of it.

The Roman values were based on the fact that everyone was able to live a life of austerity due to the smallholdings around the countryside. Roman citizens had two choices in life: to fight as a soldier or to farm the land. One never excluded the other, and there are numerous stories of soldiers and even dictators who returned to farming their lands after a war. The most famous was the legendary Cincinnatus, a dictator from the 5ᵗʰ century BCE. He even gave his name to the modern-day city of Cincinnati in the United States.

Greek culture introduced a life of softness and leisure to the aristocracy. Rome entered a social crisis, where the aristocracy ignored the power of the Senate and indulged in corruption and bribery.

Social Troubles

Some Roman citizens didn't accept the new way of life that called for pleasure, leisure, and corruption. There was a rising call for social reforms among individuals who enjoyed orgies, brothels, and private parties of the aristocracy. The most vocal among them were two brothers: Tiberius and Gaius Sempronius Gracchus. They quickly realized this Greek influence was not only affecting high society but also the economy of the country. Smallholdings disappeared, making way for big, industrial-type landowners. Many poor people had to leave the countryside, as it no longer offered work, and try their fortune in the large cities.

The Gracchi were a noble family. Their name is connected to five separate consuls of Rome, and the mother of Tiberius and Gaius was none other than Cornelia, the daughter of Scipio Africanus. Cornelia was considered a virtuous woman who abided by all the Roman traditions of the time, and she was determined to keep Rome true to its values. Her ambitions were transferred to her sons, and one could say Cornelia produced the first Roman reformers. In 134, Tiberius was elected as a tribune. This position gave him access to higher politics and granted him the ability to veto the acts of magistrates and the Senate. He was determined to use his power to make a change in the country and to return the land to the small landowners. He proposed that anyone who owned more land than the Roman law prescribed (120 hectares) should surrender that land, which would then be divided among the poor in small plots (7 hectares). Tiberius was clever not to touch the wealthy's private property. Only those who gathered more than what was allowed were to lose some land, and they would even go without punishment for land grabbing.

But Tiberius angered the Senate by ignoring them completely, as he never even bothered to consult with them on his reforms. Believing Tiberius to be a threat to their influence, the Senate accused him of trying to install a tyranny and had him killed. Tiberius didn't go without a fight, though. He had many supporters among the poor, who flocked around his property to protect him. A conflict occurred, which resulted in 300 dead, among them Tiberius himself.

In 124, Gaius Gracchus, the brother of Tiberius, was elected as a tribune. Although he continued his brother's efforts, he proved to be a more formidable man who could please both sides. He started by economically protecting the poor by allowing them to purchase grain and corn at fixed prices. This way, the poor wouldn't be as affected by failing crops and bad weather. He continued by pleasing the wealthier classes of Rome and getting their support. The newly acquired wealth of the recently conquered Pergamum was to be auctioned among the wealthy, and Gaius started various building projects that benefited the contractors of Rome.

It seemed that Gaius was doing everything right. He was fighting for the poor while pleasing the wealthy at the same time. The Senate had nothing against him, as he left them alone. But problems occurred when he tried to continue his brother's work of confiscating the extra land and giving it to the poor. This time, it was Rome's allied states that disagreed. They saw no benefits of the Roman law extending to them, and they weren't even pleased with the offer of Roman citizenship. Finally, the Senate had to act, as the possible influx of new citizens would create an insecure state. While Gaius was away from Rome, the Senate passed a law to create more colonies for Roman citizens in Italy. The poor liked this idea better than what Gaius had to offer, and he lost their support. He wasn't elected as a tribute the next year. By 121, he gathered a small number of followers and tried to repeal the law of the colonies. A scuffle broke out, and one of the consul's servants died. This was the excuse the Senate needed to get rid of Gaius. Seeking revenge for his servant, the consul proclaimed a prize for Gaius's head. Soon, it was delivered, and since the prize was the head's weight in gold, legend has it that it was filled with lead where the brain used to be. Just like his brother, Gaius did not go down without a fight, and the lives of 3,000 citizens were lost.

The Marian Reforms

The social problems of Rome continued, and any effort to solve them was hindered by the continuous expansion of the state. The new possessions in Numantia and Pergamum, as well as the expansion to the north in the Gallic territories, meant the Roman citizens migrated, stretching out the base from which a consul could draw his army. Up until now, the Roman army was voluntary, and each soldier had to pay for his equipment and weapons. Only the wealthiest were able to afford a horse, while the poorest couldn't even enlist in the army. This meant many citizens couldn't be farmers, as they possessed no land. They also couldn't serve in the army, as they couldn't buy weapons.

With only a handful of citizens eligible for the army, and many poor sitting idle in the cities, it was clear that some kind of social reform was needed. When the throne of Numidia was usurped by King Jugurtha in 111 BCE, Rome simply didn't have enough people to defend its property. A large part of its army was still in Asia Minor, and the others were fighting the Gauls in the north. It was clear that the war with Numidia will be prolonged.

In 107, Gaius Marius entered the elections for consul. Previously, he served as a legate under one of the previous consuls who tried to end the war with Jugurtha. Marius proposed to recruit the landless poor citizens into the army and have the state pay for their equipment. With this, the problem of the idle poor would be solved, as well as the army's manpower problem. The landless masses were attracted to Marius's proposals because they were offered regular pay as professional soldiers, and they were allowed to take the spoils of war as their private possessions. Their employment as a professional soldier lasted for sixteen years, but this was gradually raised later. After their initial years of servitude were over, the soldiers had the option to continue to serve for another five years as *evocati.*

The second reform introduced by Gaius Marius was the formation of a standing army. This meant that after a war was over, the soldiers would remain in the army and continue their training year-round. This reform came more out of necessity than wisdom, although it proved to be one of the ways in which the discipline and loyalty of the Roman legions were ensured. When Marius took his soldiers to Numidia and finally overthrew the usurper king, he didn't know what to do with his army, as they had no possessions to return to. At first, he offered the Senate the option to grant them land in Africa and Italy. But the Senate refused. Having no other option, Marius came up with the proposal of a standing army that would be fully dependent on the state. In turn, the army would always be ready to defend and conquer more territories.

The Senate approved of the idea of a standing army, as it would allow Rome to respond to immediate threats much faster. A commander didn't have to gather the volunteers first and train them for fighting before taking them to the battlefield. With a standing army, the commanders had soldiers at their disposal whenever a problem arose. The only remaining problem was what to do with the retired soldiers. Finally, the Senate agreed to grant the land and a pension fee to those who finished their service, but the land was only given in territories that had been recently conquered, and they were never in Italy. This way, Rome could populate newly conquered areas with their own loyal citizens, which helped to prevent uprisings and any other possible problems. The results of the Marian reforms was a large standing army that expressed only loyalty and gratitude toward their commanders. Such an army was able to lead Rome to many victories and make itself one of the most respected and known armies throughout history.

The Social War and Sulla's March on Rome

Gaius Marius's success with Numidia left Roman allies with a bitter taste in their mouths. They realized that Rome was using them to recruit soldiers among their ranks, as well as to collect taxes and food to maintain the army. However, once a new territory was conquered, they did not have the same rights as Roman citizens to enjoy the spoils of war. No captured riches were given to the allied cities, and the new lands did not belong to their citizens. Only Romans were allowed to enjoy the spoils of war. The rest were treated as second-grade citizens. The only hope to reach equality was for the allied citizens to somehow gain Roman citizenship.

In 95 BCE, the Senate passed a new law that gave the censors the power to expel anyone who falsely claimed Roman citizenship. The elite citizens of the allied cities were angered, but a new hope came in 91, when a new tribune, Marcus Livius Drusus, proposed granting citizenship to the aristocracy of the Roman allies to close the gap in numbers between the poor and rich in Rome. The allies wanted Roman citizenship more than anything, but some of them were holders of large land estates. They were worried citizenship would force them to give up some of their lands so it could be redistributed to the poor. Unfortunately, Drusus's political opponents accused him of acting out of personal interests, as he only wanted to build his own private power base. In October of the same year, he was assassinated. The hopes of the allies were crushed, and the assassination of Drusus acted as a catalyst for a revolt.

Livius Drusus wanted to please everyone, but in the end, he only managed to make the situation even tenser. After he perished, many

Italians who hoped they would get the citizenship gathered to take what they wanted by force. The leader of the initiative was a Marsian named Quintus Poppaedius Silo. Sometimes, the Social War of 91-87 is also called the Marsian War or War of Allies.

Instead of fighting Rome, twelve allied cities in the central and southern Apennines united and founded a state known as Italia (the name came about because the Greeks called the inhabitants of these cities Itali). Italia's capital was Corfinium, located in the territory east of Rome. This territory used to belong to one of the first enemies of Rome, the Samnites. There, in the first Italia, the allies founded their own senate, which numbered 500 representatives from all 12 cities, issued coinage, and started an army. In no time, they gathered an army that could easily stand up to Rome. Most of it was structured out of the deserters from the Roman army. Their numbers were around 120,000, comparable to Rome's 150,000.

Not all of Rome's allies joined the new confederation. Etruria and Umbria joined at first but quickly left the rebels. None of the Latin communities joined the confederation, as they had the most privileged status of the allied cities. Central Campania also remained loyal to Rome, and so did certain individual communities whose territories were in the rebel's lands. Even though the Roman and rebel military forces were approximately equal, Rome's access to resources proved to be superior.

The allied cities had no intention of attacking their enemy except in cases of defending themselves, and they managed to fend off the Roman attacks for a year. But during 90 BCE, the rebels managed to capture some of the Roman fortifications, and they defeated Rome on several occasions. The rebels soon became aware of Rome's superiority and realized it was just a matter of time before they were defeated for good. Still, the rebels pressured Rome with their victories, and the Senate had no other choice but to offer citizenship to the aristocracy who remained loyal to increase the number of Roman soldiers. This citizenship offer extended to all those who laid down their weapons, and soon, the rebelling allies found themselves divided.

The fighting continued throughout 89 BCE. Eventually, Rome captured Corfinium and Asculum, the last major rebel stronghold. After that, it was easy to quell the remnants of the rebellion. During this period, young Pompey gained his first military experience, as did Cicero. Both of these individuals would play an important role in Roman politics. Rome passed a second law in which citizenship was granted to individuals who were not eligible to receive it the previous year. Eventually, all the communities south of the River Po were granted Roman citizenship.

The consequences of the Social War stretched over the next several decades. This was the first time Italy experienced a full-scale civil war, and it was only a prelude to what was about to happen. For the next sixty years, Rome would go through a political horror show and would have to change, for better or worse. As for the time being, Rome changed its administrative and political status, and the new citizens gained the right to involve themselves in political life. They had the right to vote and run for various offices, which they did. But the change no one saw was the death of many regional languages and the rise of Latin throughout Italy. To be able to communicate with their new colleagues, the new citizens had to learn the language of Rome. They took it back to their home cities, where it settled and spread through all the social classes.

The new citizens constructed eight new tribes, which were added to the already existing thirty-five tribes of Rome. Even though, by law, they had the same citizenship rights as the original tribes, they were always called to vote last, meaning they had less impact on the political matters of the state. Their voting rights were also limited, which allowed the political patterns of Rome to remain undisturbed. In 88 BCE, one of the tribunes, Publius Sulpicius Rufus, wanted to make a change for the eight new tribes. He believed that the new citizens should be distributed throughout the previously existing thirty-five tribes. Publius Sulpicius Rufus never imagined that the strongest opposition to his proposal would come from Consul Lucius Cornelius Sulla, whom he previously helped win the election.

Sulla was one of Rome's most successful military generals. At first, he served under Gaius Marius and helped him defeat the usurper Jugurtha. Sulla was also known for his victories against the Germanic tribes, as well as his success in the recent Social War. Once he became the consul in 88 BCE, Sulla was given command over the army, which fought the Pontic King Mithridates VI over interests in Asia Minor. But now, Sulpicius Rufus found an unlikely ally in Gaius Marius, who wanted Sulla to be disposed of so he could take over the command of the war with Mithridates. With the help of Marius, Sulpicius Rufus managed to pass his proposal for the redistribution of voters; at the same time, Marius gained the command he desired. Sulla left Rome with his army to meet the last rebel holdout at Nola. There, he received the news that he had lost the command of the war with the Pontic king.

If Sulla accepted this, all his hard work in Roman politics would go to waste. On the other hand, if he took the law into his own hands, he would earn the resentment of the Romans. But Sulla wasn't alone. He had the loyalty of the six legions who were at Nola with him, the men he was supposed to take to Asia Minor. His soldiers adored him, and they even presented him with a crown woven of grass, called the *corona graminea*, naming him *imperator*, a title given to a commander who won a major victory.

It was a constitutional crime to bring the army to Rome to gain political demands instead of doing it through the voting system. All politically active citizens of Rome would oppose Sulla if he chose to take his command back by force. However, Sulla had no other choice, and he asked his soldiers for support. All of his commanders abandoned him, but the army remained loyal to him.

So, when Marius's officers came to take the command, they were killed. In Rome, the consuls and the Senate had never dreamed Sulla would attack the city, so they didn't prepare for the attack. This element of surprise played a major role in his victory. Once the city was his, Sulla pressured the Senate to declare Sulpicius Rufus and Marius as enemies of the state, together with nine military commanders who were on their side. This was a smart move because it created the image that his coup was legitimate. Sulla also made sure that Sulpicius Rufus's reforms were stopped and that the command of the war with Mithridates went back to him. However, this also meant there was no redistribution of voters, and the people resented Sulla for that. But once he secured the city, Sulla went to Asia Minor to lead the war against Pontus.

Although Sulpicius Rufus was killed while in exile, Marius and his son, who had the same name, reached the shores of Africa, where they were relatively safe because the veterans settled there would offer him protection. In 87 BCE, the consulship was assumed by Lucius Cornelius Cinna, who continued the policy of his predecessor, Sulpicius Rufus, to redistribute the voters. Marius came back from Africa and offered his support. Together, they raised an army and besieged Rome. When the city fell, Marius and Cinna started a bloody hunt on their opponents. Sulla was outlawed and proclaimed as an enemy of the state.

By mid-January 86 BCE, Gaius Marius died, probably of pneumonia. The Roman state was left in a crisis, and Cinna never had the opportunity to finish the reforms and redistribute the voters. His biggest problem after the death of his friend was what stance he would take regarding Sulla. He chose to treat him as an outlaw, and Lucius Valerius Flaccus, who served instead of Marius as consul, took off for Asia Minor to take Sulla's place in the war. But Sulla planned to dispatch his replacement, and soon, he abandoned his fight with Mithridates, allowing the Pontic king to escape. Instead, Sulla turned his army toward Rome once more. To sate the legion's anger for not finishing the war in Asia Minor, he spent eighteen months looting the towns and villages on his way home.

This time, though, news reached Rome in time, and Cinna began preparing defenses. The plan was to meet Sulla in Greece rather than wait for him to come to Rome and endanger the city. While preparing, Cinna was murdered at the port of Ancona on the Adriatic Sea. His co-consul, Gnaeus Papirius Carbo, recalled the army that had already been sent to Greece, as he decided the fight with Sulla should take place in Italy. At this critical point, Carbo finally passed the law to redistribute the voters.

In the spring of 83 BCE, Sulla arrived at Brundisium (modern-day Brindisi), leading five legions. He was immediately joined by two of Cinna's and Carbo's political opponents: Marcus Licinius Crassus and Gnaeus Pompeius (better known as Pompey). At the age of only twenty-three, Pompey had three legions of his private army, which he now put at Sulla's disposal. All of Italy was against them, as they still remembered Sulla's first march on Rome. However, most of the military generals preferred not to fight and instead tried to negotiate with the trio. The prolonged diplomatic approach angered the opponent's army, and Sulla's force swelled up with deserters. Sulla promised he changed his mind over the redistribution of the voters, swearing he would not veto the new law. However, it should be noted his hatred for the Samnites was great, as they stubbornly rebelled against Rome, and they stayed opposed to him until the very end.

The conflict between the Roman armies occurred in 82 BCE when Carbo was again elected as consul. His co-consul was supposed to be Gaius Marius, the son of Gaius Marius, the reformer of the army. However, Sulla won the conflict quickly, and the young Marius was killed. This victory practically destroyed any opposition Sulla, Crassus, and Pompey had in Italy, but Sicily and the possessions in Africa were still against them. To appease these

Roman provinces, Pompey was sent to win them back with such devastation that he earned the nickname "Young Butcher." Sulla was pleased with Pompey's efficiency, and he gave him his stepdaughter in marriage. He even allowed his young son-in-law a triumphal entrance to Rome, naming him Magnus ("the Great").

Sulla remained in power as a consul until the year 79 BCE. He decided to retire to his countryside villa but returned to politics occasionally, mainly to defend the reforms he enforced. Sulla stayed true to his promise and allowed the redistribution law to remain in power, which only brought him more support from the citizens of Rome. Sulla died in 78 BCE, leaving future politicians and military leaders an example of how to grasp power. He inspired future generations such as Pompey and Caesar, who would walk directly in the steps of Lucius Cornelius Sulla.

The First Triumvirates, Caesar, and the End of the Republic

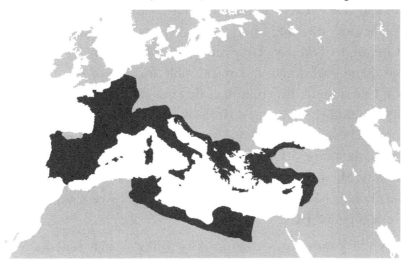

The Roman Territories before the death of Julius Caesar
TheDastanMR, CC BY-SA 4.0 <https://creativecommons.org/licenses/by-sa/4.0CC BY-SA 4.0 Creative Commons Attribution-Share Alike 4.0>, via Wikimedia Commons https://commons.wikimedia.org/wiki/File:Roman_Republic_44_bC.svg

Pompey continued to rise in power after the death of his father-in-law, Sulla. He proved himself as a great military leader, and he was allowed a second triumph for his quelling of Spartacus's slave revolt (73–71 BCE). Crassus became jealous of Pompey. Throughout Sulla's rule, Pompey remained his favorite, and even after his death, young Pompey continued to be adored among the Senate and Roman people. When Crassus was elected as consul along with Pompey in 70 BCE, everyone expected them to clash. However, the two rivals managed to work together on some of the main issues the Roman Republic faced. Once their year of consulship was over, the two staged a public reconciliation and went their separate ways, searching for the opportunity that would allow them to continue being politically involved. One such chance arose for Pompey in 67 BCE when piracy in the Mediterranean reached its peak. Since Rhodes, Egypt, and Syria were weak, it fell on Rome to deal with this Mediterranean problem.

In early 67 BCE, Pompey became a proconsul, which gave him a certain level of power that was limited to the Mediterranean region. He was also given an army with twenty legates who were propraetors, meaning they could act independently while still answering to Pompey. He divided the Mediterranean region into zones, and each legate was responsible for one of them. Pompey took Cilicia under his control, as that was the area that attracted the largest number of pirates. It took him only three months to completely remove the threat, and he once again emerged as the hero of the masses. The very next year, Pompey was sent to end the war with Mithridates VI once and for all. After successfully dealing with Pontus, Pompey continued to annex Syria and captured Jerusalem in 63 BCE.

While Pompey was away in Asia Minor, a new statesman and military general entered the Roman political scene. He was the nephew of Gaius Marius and came from a patrician family that claimed descent from the mythical Trojan prince Aeneas, whose descendants founded Rome. This was none other than the famous Gaius Julius Caesar (100–44 BCE). When Pompey returned, Caesar was in great personal debt, and he had to turn to Crassus for help. In turn, Crassus asked for his support against Pompey, his political enemy. But before Caesar had to take any immediate action against Pompey, he left for Spain, where he was given the governorship over the western part of the Iberian Peninsula. He was victorious against some of the remaining rebelling tribes, and he gained the support of his legions, who proclaimed him *imperator.* Caesar returned to Rome in 60 BCE, and the Senate allowed him a triumph. His goal was to become a consul for 59 BCE. However, Senator Cato the Younger denied him the possibility of running for office while he was away from Rome. The law was that a returning general who was allowed a triumph had to wait for the ceremony to step into the city again. But Caesar had no time, as the consulship registration couldn't wait. What Caesar did next shocked Rome. A triumph was the biggest prestige any Roman could ever aspire to. Caesar gave up his triumph to enter the city and register himself as a candidate for the consulship. Everyone was shocked that a Roman citizen would deny his triumph, but Caesar was so popular that he would easily win the elections. However, things changed quickly, and it would be uncertain if he could win the next year.

At this point, Caesar was in good relations with both Pompey and Crassus, and to secure their support in the consul elections, he needed to act as a mediator between the two political enemies. They unofficially agreed to help each other's political careers. Together, they were the most powerful group in Rome, as Pompey was a famous military general, and Crassus was regarded as the richest person in Rome. Caesar, on the other hand, had political influence. This alliance is known as the First Triumvirate, and it was sealed with the marriage between Pompey and Caesar's daughter, Julia.

During his consulship, Caesar largely ignored the Senate and his co-consul, Marcus Calpurnius Bibulus, and proceeded with the acts he thought were necessary. He passed the law of land distribution and ratified Pompey's arrangements in Asia Minor. Furthermore,

Caesar was given command over the legions who fought in Gaul for five years instead of the usual one. This way, he was able to escape the prosecution he would surely face for the misconduct during his consulship. All of the First Triumvirate's immediate goals were fulfilled during 59 when Caesar was a consul, but in the long run, this alliance would prove to be unreliable.

From 58 to 51 BCE, Caesar campaigned in Gaul, leading six legions in total. By 57 BCE, he managed to bring most of France and Belgium under his domination. In 56, the Atlantic coast and the far northwest fell under his control too. He didn't yet engage the central territory of the Gauls, but they were now surrounded and unable to unite with their western relatives. Instead of attacking the center of Europe, Caesar decided he should seek military achievements somewhere else. His goal was southern England, and in 55, he crossed the channel. Unfortunately, he was unable to organize a full-scale invasion in England, as the Gallic-Germanic tribes, the Eburones and Belgae, stirred unrest. Throughout much of 53, Caesar was trying to suppress the northern Gauls. During this time, in the central territories, Prince Vercingetorix of the Arverni arose and began a rebellion against Roman rule.

Caesar was successful in conquering the Gallic territories, as he was able to divide the leaders of various tribes. However, Vercingetorix realized the only way to defeat the Romans was to unite. Unfortunately, the unification of the Gallic tribes came too late. Vercingetorix won the early Battle of Gergovia in 52 BCE, in which thousands of Romans lost their lives. But Caesar was able to defeat the Gallic forces at Alesia (today's Alise-Sainte Reine, France). To save his people, the Gallic leader surrendered to Caesar and remained his prisoner for the next five years. He was killed by strangulation during Caesar's triumph in 46 BCE. The modern estimates believe that Caesar's conquest of the Gauls cost one million Gallic lives, while another million was enslaved.

Back in Rome, the political scene was collapsing. Various rivalries led the city to the brink of another civil war. To prevent this, the Senate wanted to levy military troops all over Italy and give Pompey a sole consulship for the year 52 BCE. A dictatorship was even discussed, but it was rejected, as Pompey was already too powerful and had too much influence over politics. At this point, Pompey passed the law that stated five years must pass for an individual who already served in the office to become a governor again. This meant that after Caesar returned from his conquest in Gaul, he needed to become a private citizen for five years before he would be able to run for office again. It would ruin his political career, as his enemies would have enough time to collect and bring up charges against him. Caesar thought he would be exempted from the rule since he was Pompey's ally, but his daughter Julia, who was married to Pompey, died in 54 BCE. Pompey had no ties to Caesar now, and he was seeking to undermine his opponent. This hostility between the two ex-allies continued through 51 and 50 BCE, and the overall sense of brewing civil war enveloped Rome.

To avoid military clashes between Caesar and Pompey, the Senate voted that both of them should give up their commands over the legions. The consuls for that year didn't agree, and they vetoed the Senate, which left Pompey with two legions stationed at Campania. He was also authorized to raise as many soldiers as he needed to defend Rome from a possible attack by Caesar. Pompey's acceptance of the consuls' wishes pushed him to finally declare himself as Caesar's enemy. The search for a compromise continued through 49 BCE, as Caesar's friend, Gaius Scribonius Curio, who was also a legate, made connections with the two tribunes: Quintus Cassius Longinus and Marcus Antonius (Mark Antony). When the Senate called for a vote over Caesar disbanding his army or else being proclaimed an enemy of the state, the proposal was instantly vetoed by Cassius Longinus and Mark Antony. However, these two tribunes were threatened, and they had to run away from Rome to save their lives. They met with Caesar in the north.

Because it was wintertime, Pompey and the senators didn't expect any further

developments to occur, and they didn't realize what the sudden flight of Mark Antony and Cassius Longinus might mean for them. So, Rome was unprepared when Caesar led his legions across the River Rubicon on January 10th, 49 BCE. This river was a borderline between the lands of the Gauls and the Romans, and Caesar had no right, by Roman law, to bring his troops over the river. The fact that he did it meant he was ready to engage in a civil war. His supposed words as he crossed the river were *Alea iacta est* ("the die has been cast"). This meant there was no turning back, and it was up to destiny. In Caesar's view, the Senate was disrespectful, and it wasn't their place to dictate his future. He was a senior senator and an outstanding military commander; it was not right for them to ruin his political career like this. But, of course, he didn't voice his view out loud, but he did put it to pen. Caesar justified his march on Rome as a defense of the Roman constitution, which the Senate and the consuls were breaking.

While marching toward Rome, Caesar barely encountered any resistance. The entire region of Picenum supported Caesar and his cause, and while the people of Corfinium tried to fight him, the city's army forced their general to surrender. Caesar never took a prisoner, and he didn't execute anyone. He also declined to take the treasuries of the cities that surrendered to him, which made the people believe his cause was just and that he didn't do anything for his own gain. Pompey's position was uncertain, as rumors arose that he had no loyalty amongst his troops. Instead of confronting Caesar, Pompey decided to flee to Greece, abandoning not just the city but the whole of Italy. His move was seen as a defeat by the people of Rome, but he actually planned to raise armies beyond Roman borders and then invade Rome. The city was open for the taking.

After spending two weeks in Rome, Caesar knew he needed to act fast and prevent Pompey from gathering an army. His first goal was to tackle the concentration of Pompey's troops in Spain, and by fall, he had completed his mission. In 48 BCE, Caesar decided to pursue Pompey in the east. There, Caesar was almost defeated, but instead of allowing Pompey to destroy his army, Caesar decided to flee. Now it was Pompey's turn to pursue Caesar. In August, a major battle occurred at Thessaly, and Pompey was defeated, despite having a larger army. Caesar offered forgiveness to whoever asked for mercy, and many did. Pompey's grip on the Mediterranean region and the eastern provinces was over. He decided to seek refuge in Ptolemaic Egypt, but he met his death as soon as he landed. Pharaoh Ptolemy XIII, believing this move would please Caesar, had sent assassins.

Caesar pursued Pompey and reached Alexandra only a few days later. Once Caesar arrived, he learned of his opponent's death, which he was not pleased about. Even though he had no business in Egypt, for some reason, he decided to stay and involve himself in the ongoing dynastic struggle. Because of this, he remained trapped in Egypt until 47 BCE. While in Egypt, Caesar chose to support the ambitious Cleopatra VII, and he helped her take the throne from her brother's grasp. In the meantime, Caesar and Cleopatra became lovers, which resulted in the birth of Caesar's son, Ptolemy Caesar, nicknamed Caesarion.

In 47 BCE, Caesar was finally able to return to Rome, but his opponents had taken the time to gather forces in Africa. His main opponent was Marcus Porcius Cato, also known as Cato the Younger. He was a follower of the Stoicism philosophy and a conservative senator. Rather than owing his life to Caesar, he preferred to die for his principles. When Utica surrendered without a fight in 46 BCE, Cato decided to commit suicide. Caesar then had to fight in Spain, where Pompey's sons had gathered a considerable army. By June 45 BCE, he dealt with his Pompey's sons, but the campaign in Spain proved to be one of his most difficult victories. Even after defeating all of his opponents, there was no rest for Gaius Julius Caesar. In the spring of 44 BCE, he planned on going to war against the Parthians in Syria. Only four days before his departure, Caesar was assassinated by the senators of Rome. This occurred on March 15th, a sacred date that Romans considered perfect for returning debts. Around sixty men were involved in the killing, and Caesar was stabbed twenty-three times. Among the perpetrators was his personal friend, Marcus Junius Brutus, who became one of the most famous of Caesar's killers. Even today, his name is a synonym for betrayal. Brutus turned against his friend because he realized Caesar was taking too much power into his own hands. He joined the conspiracy, and according to historical accounts of the event, he was among the last to stab Caesar.

Even though he was away from Rome most of the time, Caesar did much for the city. He raised the standard of living for the poor by employing them to work on his building projects, such as the Forum Julium (also known as the Forum of Caesar) and the Saepta Julia (the Romans' voting site). None of these projects were done during his lifetime. To further reduce unemployment, Caesar offered a fresh start for the poor in the newly conquered provinces, which many gladly accepted. To relieve hunger, he built a new harbor in Ostia and a canal from Terracina, by which grain was securely transported from Egypt to Rome. Rome proved loyal to Caesar, and he had grandiose plans to repay the people for it. He wanted to make Rome the cultural center of Italy, where all the prominent people of the Mediterranean world would flock. Unfortunately, he didn't live long enough to fulfill his intentions, and we can only speculate what Rome would have become had he lived just a bit longer.

The Second Triumvirate and the Transformation of Rome

Gaius Octavius, the eighteen-year-old nephew of Caesar, was studying in Apollonia, Illyricum (Illyria), when the news of his uncle's death reached him. He left immediately, intending to return to Rome and start his political career. He was accompanied by his close friend, Marcus Vipsanius Agrippa, who would remain at Octavius's side as long as he lived. Gaius Octavius had the opportunity to meet Caesar, and he developed a close relationship with his uncle while accompanying him on his Spanish campaign in 45 BCE. The two were so close that Caesar decided to adopt young Octavius and make him his official heir. However, Octavius was unaware of this until he reached Brundisium in Italy. Once in Rome, Caesar's young nephew officially accepted his inheritance and took the name Gaius Julius Caesar Octavianus to honor his uncle. Of course, this name had an intimidating effect on his political enemies, but it also created an instant connection between Octavianus and the people. He needed this connection since he was young and had no political support. To distinguish himself from Caesar, modern historians prefer to use Octavian when referring to Gaius Julius Caesar Octavianus.

Because Octavian was so young and inexperienced, Mark Antony didn't see him as a political threat. But the nephew of Caesar showed extreme political prowess. In his will, Caesar left 300 sesterces (ancient Roman silver coins) to each Roman citizen, but Antony was reluctant to fulfill this part of the will, and he came up with various reasons not to release the money. To secure the support of the people, Octavian sold his estate to pay the people. Antony quickly realized that Octavian, even though he was only eighteen years old, was a greater enemy than he could ever imagine. Octavian used his name and the memory of the great Caesar to gain not just the love of people but also the support of various politicians who still respected his uncle. Soon, Antony gave up his intentions to politically ruin young Octavian, and he decided to take up the governorship of Cisalpine Gaul in northern Italy.

But Cicero and the Senate of Rome still considered Mark Antony an enemy of the state for his loyalty to Caesar. They plotted to get rid of him, and they even approached Octavian for help. While young Octavian was adopted as the son of Caesar, and he took up his uncle's name and used the memory of him to manipulate the people of Rome, the Senate still considered him the lesser evil, a boy who would be easily manipulated. In the meantime, Octavian gathered a large private army, which the Senate wanted to use against Antony. In 43 BCE, a conflict occurred at Mutina (modern-day Modena), the capital of Cisalpine Gaul at the time. Mark Antony was defeated, and Octavian gained a position in the Senate as a subordinate to the office of the consul.

Both consuls, Aulus Hirtius and Gaius Vibius Pansa Caetronianus, were killed during the conflict at Mutina, and Octavian demanded to be proclaimed a consul as a reward for his efforts against Mark Antony. However, the Senate refused him because he was simply too young for that position. The young Octavian refused to pursue Antony, even though the Senate ordered him to. Instead, Octavian chose to send his representatives to Rome to demand consulship, but they were refused. Octavian was only nineteen when he marched on Rome, leading his eight legions. That was enough to scare the senators, and he was given the position of a consul on August 19th, 43 BCE. His co-consul was his relative, another nephew of Caesar, Quintus Pedius.

As a consul, Octavian had the power to deal with the assassins of his uncle Caesar. They were all outlawed and condemned for their actions. In the meantime, Mark Antony escaped to the north, where he met with Caesar's supporter Marcus Aemilius Lepidus. With only a bit of persuasion, the two Caesarians (those who supported Caesar during his lifetime) allied. But Octavian wasn't interested in conflict anymore, and with Lepidus as a mediator, he reconciled with Antony. The three men formed what would later be known as the Second Triumvirate. This newfound friendship would last for the next five years.

In contrast to the First Triumvirate, the second one was legal. The arrangements were concluded in Bononia (today's Bologna) in October of 43 BCE. By November, the Roman Senate had adopted it as a law. The three members of the Triumvirate gained the power to make laws without consulting the Senate or the Roman people. They were also able to nominate the magistrates and to execute jurisdictional powers without appeal. They were essentially dictators in all but name. However, to keep the opposition satisfied, the members of the Triumvirate continued consulting the public when they wanted to implement major changes in Roman law.

The Triumvirate also gained the governorship of some of the territories. Antony took responsibility for Cisalpine and Transalpine Gaul, Lepidus for Spain and Narbonese Gaul, while Octavian took Africa, Sicily, and Sardinia. The first and most important task of the Triumvirate was to pursue the assassins of Caesar. For this task, Antony and Octavian were given command of over twenty legions each. This number represented a third of all the Roman legions in existence at this time. But commanding the legions wasn't the problem; the trouble began when both Octavian and Antony lacked the money to pay their soldiers. To keep their army, the members of the Triumvirate had to come up with the money quickly, and they started condemning their political enemies and taking their riches. Among them was Cicero, who was caught and killed in his villa outside of Rome. But this wasn't enough, and soon, both Antony and Octavian started handing whole cities over to the army. In total, eighteen cities and the territories around them provided for the military needs of Rome.

The Senate decided to posthumously proclaim Julius Caesar as a state divinity, and this was officially done on January 1ˢᵗ, 42 BCE. On this occasion, the month in which Caesar was born was renamed July in his honor. Octavian started calling himself *Divi filius* ("son of a god"), which allowed him to pursue political advantages. With the new year came a new task for the Triumvirate, and Mark Antony's and Octavian's armies were sent to fight against Brutus and Gaius Cassius Longinus, two of Caesar's assassins. The pair had built a power base in Greece, and Rome sent twenty-eight legions in total to fight them. Octavian refused to go, giving the command of his troops to his friend Agrippa. For this, Antony would later mock him, calling Octavian a coward and emphasizing how the victory was only achieved because of his leadership skills.

Two battles occurred in Macedonia, near Philippi (near Thasos). During the first battle, Brutus defeated Octavian's army, but Cassius lost to Antony and committed suicide. The second battle started well for Brutus, but the joint forces of Antony and Octavian were too much, and his front defenses broke. After the defeat, Brutus committed suicide. With Brutus, the republican cause came to an end, as he was the last Roman who still refused to admit that Rome was changing. After the battle, the Triumvirate redistributed control over the territories, and Antony chose Egypt as his seat of power. There, he would ally with Queen Cleopatra VII, the former lover of Caesar. Octavian was now in control of Spain and Gaul, while Lepidus took Africa.

Since Octavian promised the veterans of Philippi lands on which to settle, he evicted more cities to give them to the military. In total, twenty-three cities were emptied, and they became military properties. This angered innocent people who lost their homes and possessions. In the meantime, Sextus Pompey, Pompey the Great's son, gathered his forces and blocked the grain import in Rome. The dissatisfied citizens rebelled when famine hit Rome, and a new civil war started. Dissatisfied with Octavian, the people of Rome gave their support to Lucius Antonius, the brother of Mark Antony. Lucius, together with Mark Antony's wife Fulvia, started a campaign against Octavian. They raised an army and fought Octavian at Perusia (today's Perugia) but were unable to win. Octavian spared their lives and forgave them since they were relatives of his Triumvirate colleague Mark Antony. Antony, who was in Egypt, was aware of the events happening in Rome. He chose to remain indifferent and see what the outcome would be. Of course, he would benefit if Octavian lost, but he didn't want to estrange the Romans by directly meddling in the domestic struggle from faraway Egypt.

The tension between the members of the Triumvirate continued, and both Antony and Octavian sought to reach an agreement. They met at Brundisium in September of 40 BCE. To seal the peace between them, Octavian gave his sister Octavia in marriage to Mark Antony, as Fulvia had recently died. Octavian took it upon himself to deal with the matter of Sextus Pompey, and he agreed to marry his sister, Scribonia, to appease his enemy, who would, in turn, open the blockade of grain. Scribonia was much older than Octavian, and this was her third marriage. Nevertheless, she managed to give Octavian his only child, a daughter named Julia. The couple divorced a year after their wedding.

The divorce of his sister angered Pompey, especially when Octavian decided to marry Livia Drusilla on January 17th, 38 BCE, only days after his daughter with Scribonia was born. She was previously married to Tiberius Claudius Nero, her cousin and the enemy of Octavian. With her marriage to Octavian, the Claudius and Julius families united, paving the road for the future Julio-Claudian dynasty. With Pompey as an immediate threat, Octavian had to find allies to fight him, as his forces alone were not enough. He reached out to Antony and Lepidus once again, and an agreement was stuck to prolong the Triumvirate for another five years.

Agrippa became the consul in 37 BCE, and it was on him to lead the forces against Sextus Pompey. Lepidus promised the help of his African troops, but the beginning of the war didn't go well for Octavian's forces, and the conflict continued into the next year. In 36 BCE, Agrippa's command over the naval forces proved to be superior, as he won a series of battles on the sea. The decisive battle occurred near Naulochus, where 300 ships on each side engaged in fighting on September 3rd. Pompey was defeated and fled to Asia Minor. He was finally caught and executed in Miletus (in today's Turkey).

Lepidus wanted Sicily for himself, and after the battle with Pompey, he ordered Octavian to leave. But his army was easily persuaded to join Octavian once they were promised money as a reward. Octavian's army was now reinforced by Lepidus's defectors and the defeated soldiers of Pompey's army. With such power, Octavian was able to humiliate Lepidus, remove him from the Triumvirate, and take his possessions in Africa. Lepidus was forced to live in exile at his villa in Circeo. However, since he was still an important Roman politician, he was allowed to keep his position as a senator and as pontifex maximus (chief high priest of the College of Pontiffs), but it was only in name. He had no executive powers, and he was unable to ever return to Rome.

Octavian against Mark Antony and Cleopatra

To successfully explain the conflict between Rome and Egypt, we must trace the developments in the east that would lead to the end of the Triumvirate and the suicide of two lovers. Antony decided to make his permanent residency in Egypt after the victory at Philippi in 42 BCE. This choice wasn't an accident. Antony wanted to continue the offensive against Parthia (the northern territories of today's Iran), an endeavor started by his old friend Caesar. For this, he wanted to make an ally of Egyptian Queen Cleopatra VII, as she ruled the biggest independent state of the eastern Mediterranean. To organize the alliance, Antony scheduled a meeting with the Egyptian queen at Tarsus in Cilicia in 41 BCE. However, this wasn't the first time they met. While still being Caesar's lover, Cleopatra resided in Rome for a short time, but she had to leave for her safety and the safety of her son Caesarion after Caesar's assassination.

The alliance between Antony and Cleopatra quickly developed into an intimate relationship. The Egyptian queen gave birth to twins, a boy and a girl, only a year after meeting Antony, and the pair took up residency in Alexandria. But Antony did not settle for the domestic life in Egypt. He engaged in the internal struggle of Egypt and helped Cleopatra strengthen her rule. Even though he admitted the twins were his children, he never married Cleopatra. At the time, he was still married to Fulvia, who would soon die. To seal the agreement with Octavian, he was forced to marry Octavia, who stayed in Rome once Antony returned to Egypt.

In the spring of 40 BCE, Mark Antony departed to take the command over the defenses in the Parthian invasion. The Parthians wanted to conquer Asia Minor and Syria. Unfortunately, the development of the events between Sextus Pompey and Octavian required Antony's presence in Italy. He was forced to leave Egypt and the conflict with Parthia. In the fall of 37 BCE, once the matter with Octavian was resolved, Antony returned to the east, and Cleopatra joined him in Syria. The next year, the famous lovers had another child, a son, who Antony gladly recognized as his own.

History doesn't have a true insight into the relationship between Cleopatra and Mark Antony. They were lovers, but it is not known if it was true love or if each was driven by their personal goals. The situation is even more complicated due to the lack of evidence regarding Cleopatra's plans for the future of her kingdom. The relationship was public, and everyone in Rome knew about it. Mark Antony never bothered to hide it from his wife or her powerful brother, Octavian. But one thing is certain. If he planned to divorce Octavia and marry Cleopatra, that marriage would never be recognized by Roman law. It was simply unheard of and against the law for a high-ranking Roman citizen to be married to a foreigner.

In Parthia, Antony took the opportunity of the erupting civil war that followed their king's abdication. Initially, he won some of the battles and took his troops deep into the Parthian territory. However, his ally, the king of Armenia, decided to leave the battle and take his cavalry. Antony was defeated and forced to retreat with only one-third of his army. In contrast to his defeat, Octavian was victorious against Pompey in the same year, and the two members of the Triumvirate essentially switched roles. Octavian was now the one with the military prestige, while Antony had nothing to return to. So, he chose to go to Egypt again.

With the expulsion of Lepidus from the Triumvirate, Rome had two rulers: Octavian in the west and Antony in the east. But the divided rule couldn't last for long. The race for the sole rule over Rome began. Octavian had to improve his military prestige, and in the years to come, he undertook a series of campaigns against the tribes in Illyricum (35–33 BCE). These conflicts were supposed to keep his troops busy and trained while he undertook the task of spreading propaganda against Antony and Cleopatra. Unfortunately, Antony had no time to respond to Octavian, as he was busy with the situation developing in the eastern territories. He subdued Armenia, which served as a bridge between his forces and Parthia. During the course of 35 and 34 BCE, he finally managed to lead a successful invasion of Parthia, even though he was humiliated by Octavian. Under the ruse of sending him reinforcements, Octavian sent his sister Octavia to join her husband in the east. Antony couldn't allow his wife to meet his lover, Cleopatra. Instead, he ordered Octavia to remain in Athens. Octavian used his sister's unfortunate marriage to prove to the public that Antony had abandoned Roman virtues. However, neither side pursued a divorce.

In Egypt, Antony decided to ignore Octavian and Rome. He gave the newly conquered territories in the east, which, by law, were now Roman possessions, to Cleopatra and her children (those by him and Julius Caesar). In 33 BCE, he finally became aware that Octavian's propaganda was working. Antony realized a clash with Octavian was unavoidable, and he started preparing his troops, which were now reinforced by the Egyptians. Together, the couple brought their troops to Greece, where Antony's commanders urged him to send Cleopatra back to Egypt to improve his standing with

Rome. But Antony refused, as he was afraid the Egyptian queen would take her ships and troops with her. During this period, Mark Antony finally decided to divorce Octavia. He thought it was better if he initiated the separation instead of waiting for her brother, Octavian, to demand it, as that would ruin his image in Rome completely.

In Rome, Octavian wanted to ferret out the supporters of Mark Antony among the politicians. He came to the Senate with an armed escort. This act offended and scared some of the senators, who fled to Antony under the excuse that Octavian couldn't be trusted since he was willing to bring the army into the Senate. But Octavian still needed justification for his moves against Antony. To provide evidence that Antony had abandoned Rome, he stole his will and made it public. In the will, Antony supposedly arranged for his burial in Alexandria, and he even ensured a large part of his riches would be inherited by Cleopatra's children. However, Octavian wasn't sure if he had the support of the people, so he made civilians swear an oath of loyalty to him. He declared he would wage war against Cleopatra, leaving the name of Mark Antony out of it. By this, he avoided declaring a civil war, as he was afraid of losing the people's love and support. In late 32 BCE, Octavin convinced the Senate to revoke Antony's consular powers and to declare war against Egypt under the pretense of defending the nation against Cleopatra's regime.

At Actium, in western Greece, the large forces of Octavian and Mark Antony clashed in early 31 BCE. Under the leadership of Agrippa, the Octavian fleet was victorious. On land, Octavian himself led his forces southward to trap the lovers, who found themselves surrounded. In September, Cleopatra fled directly to Egypt, while Antony took the route through Libya. Both of them left their armies at the mercy of Octavian. The fighting stopped, but Octavian never fully gave up on pursuing Antony. He continued gathering and preparing his forces, and in the next year, 30 BCE, he led an assault on Alexandria. Antony's army deserted him, and the city fell without much resistance.

The events that followed remain mysterious, as it is hard to discern historical fact from the various legends about the famous lovers. Mark Antony committed suicide, but it remains unknown if he did it because of his imminent defeat or because he heard false news that Cleopatra had killed herself. Whatever the case was, the Egyptian queen was still alive, and she was captured by Octavian, who decided to spare her. However, only nine days later, Cleopatra took her own life. Whether she couldn't bear the humiliation of losing to Octavian or whether she couldn't continue living without Mark Antony, we will never know. Octavian couldn't allow her son by Caesar to continue living, as he posed a direct threat to his claims as Caesar's heir. The boy was executed, but Cleopatra's children by Mark Antony were allowed to live.

Now with the wealth of Egypt in his hands, Octavian annexed Egypt and made it a Roman province. At the age of thirty-three, Octavian achieved the ultimate power over Rome and its provinces. He successfully eliminated all of his rivals, and on multiple occasions, he was in danger of ending his political career. It took him fourteen years to achieve his ambition of ruling Rome. The fact that no one was able to dispose of him for the next forty-one years speaks further about his ability to control the people and the events around him.

Chapter 5 – Pax Romana

What followed the defeat of Mark Antony and the annexation of Egypt was a peace that lasted for more than 200 years. However, this doesn't mean Rome never went to war. The few revolts that occurred just never escalated enough to involve the whole nation. Instead, they were quickly dealt with, at least on a local level. Rome still continued its expansion politics, but the series of rulers that followed managed to keep the civil disturbance at a minimum. Rome did not experience another civil war during this period of peace, known in history as the *Pax Romana.*

The conflict between Octavian and Antony was the last war of the Roman Republic, as the republic soon ceased to exist. Augustus (Octavian) became the sole ruler of Rome, but he had the difficult task of persuading the people that peace was better than war. The Romans were used to achieving personal goals and gains during times of war. Constant fighting was what secured the nation's prosperity. But through vigorous propaganda, Augustus and his descendants were able to prove the benefits of peace. Officially, the peace lasted until the death of Marcus Aurelius, the last of the "Five Good Emperors." After this, the glory of Rome started deteriorating, and eventually, war tore the state into two parts. But that is a story for the future. At this point, it is crucial to explain how the Roman Republic turned into the Roman Empire and how one man "restored the republic" while taking the sole rulership of Rome for himself.

Augustus (r. 27 BCE-14 CE)

Statue of Augustus
https://commons.wikimedia.org/wiki/File:Statue-Augustus.jpg

Octavian Gaius Caesar was never an emperor in today's meaning of the word. At the beginning of the book, we already explained that the Latin word *imperator* means commander. To hold the imperium in Rome meant to have the command over the whole country. The imperium was held by the consuls, and since the position lasted for only one year, the imperium was thought of as command, not a rule. But what happens if one person held the imperium indefinitely, which is what Octavian's aspiration was? That person then becomes *princeps* (plural *principes*), meaning "the first among all." Principes are still not the emperor in the modern understanding of the word, but it is close. Switching Rome from a republic to an empire wasn't an easy task. People resented the monarchy, and they never wanted to see a sole ruler again. This is why Octavian had to come up with new ways of keeping all the power in his own hands, and he did it in a series of genius political moves.

The Second Triumvirate probably ended around 33 BCE, and it hadn't been renewed since then. But after dealing with Mark Antony, Octavian continued to hold power and act as a triumvir. He closely approached the hated role of monarch, and he realized the dangers of it. The republic-oriented citizens of Rome wouldn't allow him to keep the power. Therefore, Octavian had to pretend he didn't want to rule, that he wasn't interested in a dictatorship or monarchy. Instead, he presented himself as the restorer of the Roman Republic. He started spreading propaganda that the conflict with Mark Antony wasn't a struggle for power but a fight for republican principles and values, which were endangered by their enemies. This victory brought him the consulship, alongside his loyal friend Agrippa. Since the year 31 BCE, Octavian had been elected as a consul each year, and no one could contest such irregularity. He was simply too powerful, and the senators knew they had to keep him pleased. Octavian had the loyalty of his many legions, but above all, he was the richest person in Rome. Money equals power, and the senators were afraid of being in the opposition.

The consulship wasn't secure enough for Octavian. As soon as someone else showed up on the political scene and grabbed the attention and support of the people and military, Octavian would be done. In ancient Rome, the only way for an individual to gain power was through politics and military achievements, so it wasn't unlikely a rival would appear soon. Therefore, Octavian needed to secure his position in some way. To achieve his goals, he staged a return of all the provinces and military command back to the Senate in 27 BCE. This showed the people that he had no intention of ruling and that he was instead an advocate for the republic. In turn, the

Senate offered him governance of the most problematic provinces, as he was the only one capable of controlling them. Octavian, a victor of the civil wars, was seen as a savior and the most capable military commander. Because of frequent unrest, the provinces of Cilicia, Gaul, Hispania, Cyprus, and Egypt had most of the Roman legions stationed in them. By acquiring the governorship of these provinces, Octavian gained command of the majority of the Roman army. The power was back in his hands without the people realizing it was all just a staged ruse. This agreement between Octavian and the Senate is known as the "First settlement."

Under the consulship of Octavian, the Senate had no executive power, and everything had to be approved by Octavian himself. He was a ruler in everything but name. For his excellency in the war and as a consul, the Senate awarded him the title Augustus on January 16th, 27 BCE. Augustus was a title with a religious connotation, as it means "the illustrious." He was also officially given the title princeps. The English word for prince originated from this Latin word. Although these titles did not officially grant him the rulership, they symbolized that he was, above all, almost regal by nature and certainly of the divine line of Caesar. Octavian's supporters wanted him to dress in royal purple and wear a golden diadem, which was a symbol of power. However, he was afraid he would estrange the people of Rome, and he refused.

Octavian Augustus wasn't a conventional ruler. He was aware he could never survive the game of politics without the support of the Senate. Although the Senate had little to no executive power, the image that it still functioned as a republican political body was of the utmost importance. Augustus never gave direct orders. Instead, he preferred to call them suggestions and councils. Even though the Senate always did what Octavian "suggested," they had the sense the decision was only theirs, which was enough. Rome continued to function as a republic, even though that was just an outside layer. If one scratched deeper, one could see Rome was turning into a real empire, ruled by only one person who had the ultimate power.

In 23 BCE, Augustus experienced a serious illness, one that made him think his days were over. He knew it was time to deal with unfinished business. The actions he took brought many changes to Rome, which are today referred to as the "Second settlement." On July 1st, Octavian resigned his consulship and was never again elected to this position. He still kept all the authority and influence; it was just without the burden of the consulship. Octavian managed to keep all of his provinces and the imperium. The Senate granted his imperium much greater powers, the so-called *imperium maius* ("greater imperium"). This meant Octavian's imperium was above all other state officials in any province of Rome. Being superior to other officials meant he could give them legitimate orders. Augustus was finally approaching the power that is often related to emperors today. But he still couldn't call himself a monarch or a despot, as that would ruin him. Instead, he took the office of a tribune, which gave him the power to check the Senate's authority. He had the power to veto any legislation the Senate tried to pass. Octavian Augustus would hold this office until his death.

Augustus was loved among the common people of Rome, as they saw him as their greatest benefactor. And this wasn't without reason. As the richest person in Rome, Octavian often invested in projects that improved Rome as a whole. He took it upon himself to finish many building projects for which the Senate had declined funding. He cared for the poor and was generous with alms. Because of this, Roman citizens were shocked when he gave up the consulship. In 22 BCE, they begged him to take the consulship for life, but this was because the commoners didn't know how greatly he benefited from the Second settlement. In their opinion, the consulship was the highest possible rank, and Octavian should have it. But that position would only hold his authority back. With the

Second settlement, Octavian was able to rule with all the power he needed. He was the ultimate *imperator*, and no one could veto him. Nevertheless, the people rioted in 20 BCE and refused to elect a second consul, leaving the office vacant for their beloved Augustus. In 19 BCE, the Senate had approved of Augustus wearing insignias of consulship even though he didn't hold the office. This finally appeased the people of Rome.

Today, Octavian Augustus is not known as the first emperor of Rome solely because of the power he held. He chose his first name to be *Imperator Caesar divi filii Augustus* ("Emperor Caesar the Illustrious Divine Don"). Using the title for a commander as his first name, Augustus wanted to connect his persona with military victories. This was important for the Roman people. Even though he brought peace to Rome, it doesn't mean Rome never entered another war. Augustus led the expansionist policies, and he convinced the citizens of Rome that they were superior and should rule the world. In reality, war meant conquered territories, and new territories brought riches and slaves to Rome. Constant expansion kept the imperial wheel turning, and Augustus was at its center. During his rule, Rome conquered all of Hispania (both Spain and Portugal), Illyricum (today's Albania and parts of Serbia, Croatia, Bosnia, and Herzegovina), Pannonia (parts of Serbia and all of Hungary), as well as regions of today's Austria, Slovenia, Switzerland, and Bavaria. But his conquest of the world wasn't concentrated only in Europe. The African provinces continue expanding their borders to the south, much of which didn't even need military intervention. Turkey, Syria, and Judea also became Roman provinces. These territories were often won and lost, and the borders were fluid. But the Roman Empire continued to grow under the rule of Augustus's successors, and Rome could count on its military power for many centuries to come.

Julio-Claudian Dynasty

Augustus was aware of the uniqueness of his position. He held great power, but he wasn't an official monarch. Therefore, he couldn't choose his heir freely. If he was to have a successor, it would have to be someone who earned the right to inherit Augustus's powers. The most natural choice was Octavian's long-time friend Agrippa. Because of his military successes, he was a well-respected Roman citizen who had the loyalty of the whole army. He had already served as consul, on more than one occasion, which brought him necessary experience in dealing with the matters of the state. It seems that Augustus wanted Agrippa as his successor, and he even gave him his only daughter, Julia, in marriage. However, Agrippa died in 12 BCE, and Augustus had to choose among other possible heirs.

Fortunately, Agrippa's marriage with Julia produced five children, among which two were sons: Gaius and Lucius. Augustus took the boys under his wing and even formally adopted them. He also took Tiberius Claudius under consideration, his wife Livia's son from her first marriage. Tiberius was ordered to divorce his first wife and marry Agrippa's widow, his step-sister Julia. That marriage was a failure, and it is believed it was one of the reasons why Tiberius exiled himself to Rhodes. However, Gaius and Lucius died in 4 and 2 CE, respectively, and Tiberius was called back to step in as the heir of Augustus. Rumors started circulating that Livia wanted to promote her son to the position of *imperator* and that she poisoned Agrippa's children to make way for Tiberius. However, historians consider these rumors very unlikely. They were possibly nothing more than anti-Tiberius propaganda by his political enemies.

Augustus had no other choice but to officially adopt Tiberius and push him into the politics of Rome so he could earn his place as the next *imperator*. When Augustus died on August 19th, 14 CE, the transition of power to Tiberius went smoothly. With no blood relative, Augustus started what would be known throughout history as the Julio-Claudian dynasty. This dynasty gave Rome six very different emperors about whom stories are still being written. Their extravagant way of life inspired both love and hatred among the citizens of Rome and eventually led to their downfall.

Tiberius (r. 14–37 CE)

A bust of Emperor Tiberius
Carole Raddato from FRANKFURT, Germany, CC BY-SA 2.0
<https://creativecommons.org/licenses/by-sa/2.0>, via Wikimedia Commons
https://commons.wikimedia.org/wiki/File:Tiberius,_Romisch-
Germanisches_Museum,_Cologne_(8115606671).jpg

Tiberius Claudius Nero spent most of his adult life outside of Rome, and once he became the heir of Augustus, he didn't have the support of the people or friends among the politicians who would help him. Nevertheless, the will of Augustus designated him as heir, and he also had the previous emperor's name, as he had been officially adopted by Augustus. Before becoming an emperor,

Tiberius was a successful military commander. But his victories in Germania and Armenia were overshadowed by the hatred he inspired among the senators of Rome during his imperium. Much of it was due to his personality. Tiberius is often described as a very secretive and suspicious soul. He had many senators tried for treason. He would accuse them of backing a conspiracy to assassinate him or for having an affair with a member of the imperial family. If a senator was proven guilty, half of his estates and material riches would be transferred to the state, so it's very possible Tiberius had ulterior motives. By gaining all the powers of Augustus, Tiberius would come in possession of convicts' estates and material goods.

Tiberius's famous suspicion of everyone led him to rely on the Praetorian Guard, an elite section of the Roman army that served as personal guards to the imperial family. By investing the power in his beloved guards, Tiberius marked the future Rome would take. The Praetorian Guard became a powerful and influential military entity in Rome, and for the next two centuries, they would be responsible for any occurrences in Rome, even the election of future emperors. During the rule of Tiberius, one Praetorian rose above others. He was Lucius Aelius Sejanus, and he had the trust of the Roman emperor. In fact, during the early 20s CE, Tiberius handed over all major imperial decisions for him to make. This praetorian prefect greatly benefited from the trust the emperor put in him, and when Tiberius moved to Capri in 26 CE, Sejanus was the one controlling all communication between Rome and its absent princeps. In 31 CE, Sejanus was finally exposed for his intrigues and plots. He was even considered directly responsible for the death of Tiberius's son, Drusus the Younger. Sejanus was executed, but Tiberius failed to see the problem in the order of the Praetorian Guard. Instead, he believed Sejanus should be responsible for the events in Rome.

Tiberius never created a connection with the Roman people. This might have been due to the lack of support he received once

Augustus made him his heir. The people always supported the son of Tiberius's brother, Germanicus (who died in 19 CE). Because of this lack of support, Tiberius transferred the election powers to the Senate. It was now solely on the Senate to elect future praetorian prefects and consuls. The people didn't riot. Instead, they were satisfied with expressing their displeasure during the gladiator games. Because Tiberius was booed and mocked during the games, he rarely attended them. He had little love for Rome, and once he moved to Capri in 26 CE, he never returned, not even for the funeral of his mother, Livia, in 29. Until his death in 37, Tiberius remained an estranged emperor who never managed to develop a relationship with his city or its populace.

Rome welcomed the death of Tiberius Caesar Augustus (a name he took after becoming the emperor). His son had died in 23 CE, but since Tiberius respected Augustus's wish to create a Julian dynasty, he adopted Nero Julius Caesar and Drusus Caesar. However, both of them died young. The only possible candidates left for the inheritance were Tiberius Gemellus (the grandson of Tiberius Augustus) and Gaius Caesar (Caligula). But Gemellus was only a teenager at the time, and as such, he wasn't suitable to inherit the title of princeps. Therefore, Caligula was the only choice, and as soon as he grabbed power, he ordered the death of Tiberius's grandson to eliminate his competition for the rule of Rome.

Caligula (r. 37–41)

A bust representing Caligula

Although he ruled for only three years, Caligula remains one of the best-known emperors of Rome. Because of his controversial life, and some would even argue madness, Caligula continues to intrigue modern historians, writers, and filmmakers. Gaius Caesar Augustus Germanicus was born as the third and only surviving child of Roman General Germanicus Julius Caesar and Agrippina the Elder, the granddaughter of Augustus. As a child, he spent most of his time among his father's soldiers, who nicknamed him Caligula, which means a little soldier's boot, as he often dressed in a way to imitate the soldiers' uniforms.

Not much is known of Caligula's life except that all his brothers and his mother were killed during the family feud with Princeps Tiberius. However, once Tiberius lost all of his possible heirs, he invited Caligula to join him at Capri, where he would be groomed to take the role of the Roman emperor. Once the old princeps died, Caligula returned to Rome, where he was greeted with high honors and hopeful people. During the first six months of his rule, Caligula was considered a good emperor. However, at the beginning of 38, he fell ill. Modern scholars believe it was some sort of brain fever as, from this point on, the behavior of the young emperor became erratic. However, there are not enough sources about Caligula's reign to come to a firm conclusion of his rule. Perhaps the stories of his madness were exaggerated and written by his political enemies as propaganda against him. Nevertheless, it is obvious that everyone quickly changed their minds about supporting the emperor.

By 39 CE, Caligula, after quarreling with the Senate, started ruling as an autocrat. It is hard to discern the truth among the various stories of his madness, but Caligula was known for insulting Roman politics, religion, and virtues. It was rumored that he planned to elevate his favorite racehorse, Incitatus, to the position of a senator. He was also known for dressing as Roman gods and asking people to worship him. New temples were built dedicated to this Roman emperor, and in Egypt, coins were issued with Caligula represented as the sun god. He even ordered a golden statue of himself and replaced the heads of gods on statues in various temples with his own. Caligula also proclaimed his sister, Julia Drusilla, a goddess after she died in 38 CE. She was the first Roman woman to be deified. Caligula adored his sister so much that rumors began circulating, claiming he had an incestuous relationship with her. However, modern historians cannot confirm this claim.

During his reign, an economic crisis occurred. His contemporaries claim that Caligula's extravagant and lavish lifestyle emptied the imperial treasury. However, later evidence suggests this was not true because his successor, Claudius, was able to pay a large sum of money to his military supporters. Today's scholars do not know whether the Roman emperor had private finances separate from those of the state. Caligula started killing wealthy and prominent people of Rome to seize their estates. He even confiscated his soldiers' spoils of war, saying it was a donation to the state. Caligula also increased all taxes and made it mandatory for people to lend money from the state and not from anyone else, just so he could levy an interest tax. He was even accused of starting a famine by confiscating the grain boats so he could make pontoon bridges for his entertainment, which he wanted to cross with chariots.

Eventually, the resentment Caligula earned through his erratic behavior led to his assassination. The Senate and Praetorian Guard conspired against him and had him killed on January 22nd, 41 CE. The murder of his wife, Caesonia, and their infant daughter followed, but the assassins couldn't find Caligula's uncle, Claudius. He was later found hiding behind a curtain in the palace. The Praetorian Guard placed Claudius under their protection to elevate him to the position of emperor once the situation calmed.

Claudius (r. 41–54 CE)

Bust of Emperor Claudius
Naples National Archaeological Museum, CC BY 2.5
<*https://creativecommons.org/licenses/by/2.5*>, *via Wikimedia Commons*
https://commons.wikimedia.org/wiki/File:Claudius_crop.jpg

Claudius was the grandson of Mark Antony and Octavia, the sister of Emperor Augustus. When the Praetorian Guard raised him to the position of emperor, they hoped he could be easily manipulated and even replaced if a better opportunity presented itself. Claudius survived an illness when he was a child, which left him half deaf, with a stutter, and with a bad leg. His relatives often thought of him as an *idiota*, which in the Latin world meant an uneducated and ignorant person with no interests in politics. Claudius showed great interest in education; he even had the famous historian Livy as his tutor. But he was never regarded as a political threat to anyone, even though he was born into the Julio-Claudian dynasty. This negative public opinion worked in Claudius's favor, as it helped him survive many imperial schemes and intrigues, in which persons in power often assassinated their political opponents' families. Claudius survived and became an emperor. Even more, he surprised everyone with his ability to stay in power for more than thirteen years. He proved to be an able emperor, whose efficiency surpassed that of his predecessors.

Although Claudius strengthened the power of Rome by bringing representatives from faraway provinces into the Senate, he estranged the Roman elite. They felt he was taking away their prerogatives and giving them to their inferiors. But this political decision will prove to be one of the best ones for the good of Rome. By entering the Roman political scene, the province representatives made sure to keep peace in their territories. Unfortunately, the Senate considered Claudius their enemy for more than one reason. While the assassination of Caligula was ongoing, the senators of Rome wanted to return to the republic. They failed when the army installed Claudius as emperor, making the Senate resented the army. When the new emperor showed gratitude to the military by awarding them 15,000 sesterces (ancient Roman money), the senators started hating him. Claudius also showed great interest in Roman law, but by meddling in the judicial activities of the state, he took away the

Senate's duties from the senators, which they saw as the emperor taking away their dignity.

By creating enemies among the senators, Claudius was forced to constantly prove his capability to rule. He also had to defend himself from various attempts on his life. For this, many senators were executed as conspirators. These events dissatisfied the Roman elite even more. However, Claudius proved to be successful in expanding the empire. In 43 CE, he started the invasion of Britain, and he even went to the island personally to conclude the campaign. He successfully conquered Britain and was granted the title Britannicus, though he never used it. However, he did name his only son Britannicus. In 43, Claudius annexed Mauritania and in Thrace in 46. Even though he established local rule in Judea by elevating Agrippa I as the ruler there, this state was reverted to a Roman province in 44. In 47, he launched an exploratory campaign in Germany, but it is not known if he ever intended to conquer this territory.

Besides successful warfare, Claudius was famous for his building projects. He wanted to improve Roman infrastructure and provide the city with improved means of grain supply. He founded a new port, north of Ostia, to which merchants could bring grain even during the winter. He also built two new aqueducts: Aqua Claudia and Aqua Anio Novus. Special attention was paid to various roads and canals around Rome and its provinces. Claudius considered roads to be the most important part of the infrastructure, as it connected the heart of the empire with its many provinces.

In regards to his personal life, Claudius was denied happiness, even though he is remembered as a womanizer. Before his first marriage, he had two failed betrothals. His second fiancé died suddenly on the day of their marriage. Claudius divorced his first wife, Plautia Urgulanilla, due to her adulterous behavior. His second wife, Aelia Paetina, was a relative of Praetorian Pontiff Sejanus, and Claudius had to divorce her due to her adoptive brother's downfall. His third wife was Valeria Messalina, who bore him Britannicus. However, she conducted a mock marriage with Gaius Silius, and her adultery became a political liability. Claudius reluctantly divorced her, and she committed suicide. The emperor's fourth and final wife was his niece, Agrippina the Younger, the daughter of Claudius's brother Germanicus. She quickly became one of the most influential women in Rome and was awarded the title Augusta. She had a son, Nero, from a previous marriage, and she convinced Claudius to adopt him and proclaim him his successor.

Claudius died of poisoning in 54 CE. The main suspect of his murder was his wife, Agrippina. Contemporary historians describe the emperor's marriage as filled with conflicts and that he often looked at his son, Britannicus, as a possible heir. To secure the throne for her son, Agrippina poisoned the mushrooms Claudius was so fond of eating. At the time of Claudius's death, Nero was only sixteen years old.

Nero r. (54-68 CE)

Bust of Emperor Nero
cjh1452000, CC BY-SA 3.0 <https://creativecommons.org/licenses/by-sa/3.0>, via Wikimedia Commons https://commons.wikimedia.org/wiki/File:Nero_1.JPG

The last emperor of the Julio-Claudian dynasty started his reign with peace and good relations with the Senate, army, and the nobility of Rome. It is said that during the first years of his reign, he was greatly influenced by his mother, Agrippina, Praetorian Prefect Sextus Afranius Burrus, and his tutor Seneca the Younger, a famous philosopher. Agrippina kept herself busy by conducting various intrigues and court scandals. Nero wanted to get rid of her influence, so he staged a ship accident in the year 53. To gain control over his empire, he also forced Seneca into retirement (in 62 CE), and three years later, Nero drove him to suicide. Burrus died in 63, probably poisoned on Nero's orders. Nero was finally able to enjoy his power over the Roman Empire.

Unfortunately, Nero was more interested in arts than in government. While surrounded by able military commanders, who won some prestigious victories in Britain and Gallic territories, Nero indulged in acting, poetry, writing, and singing. He often performed publicly and was condemned by the elite society for it. The arts were supposed to belong to the people, and the emperor was no commoner—he was divine. This connection to the people of Rome brought him popularity.

Probably the most famous event that occurred during Nero's rule was the burning of Rome. It was even rumored the emperor himself set the city ablaze to write the greatest poem of all time. However, there is no evidence to support Nero's involvement in the arson, which damaged eleven out of the fourteen districts of Rome. The rumors started because Nero planned to build his golden residency, a palace, over the majority of the burned land. Later, he gave up on that plan and even allowed the unfortunate people of Rome who lost their homes to settle in his royal gardens. It didn't matter, though; the damage was done, and it took him years to recover his reputation. In his efforts to find a scapegoat for the burning of Rome, Nero accused the Christians, a new religious sect springing up in the Roman Empire. When he persecuted the

Christians, the Roman citizens showed support for their neighbors and not the emperor.

Nero couldn't fill the boots of Claudius, and he was a poor administrator. His predecessor expanded the empire, and Nero had trouble keeping its borders secure. Two major rebellions broke out during his reign: one in Britannia, which was led by Queen Boudica of the Iceni, and one in Judea, where the First Jewish-Roman War started (66–73, known as the Great Revolt). It was only thanks to his capable generals that Nero successfully quelled these uprisings. However, he never visited the army and never paid any attention to the military needs of the state. This made him very unpopular among the Roman soldiers.

The revolt against Nero's rule occurred in 68 CE when the governor of Gallia Lugdunensis (today's France), Gaius Julius Vindex, rebelled. He quickly gained allies among other governors. One of them was Servius Sulpicius Galba, the governor of Hispania. Vindex was killed that same year, but Galba continued the revolt and put himself forward as a choice for the emperor after Nero was deposed. Galba was proclaimed an enemy of the state. Just as it seemed the situation was under control, Praetorian Prefect Gaius Nymphidius Sabinus deflected and gave support to Nero's enemy.

The emperor decided to flee Rome, but his guards disobeyed his orders. Nero couldn't even leave the port at Ostia. Forced to return to his imperial palace, he found himself completely alone. Everyone abandoned him, from his high-ranking friends and guards to the lowest of servants. He joined his only remaining loyal friend, a freedman named Phaon, in his villa outside of Rome. There, Nero decided to die. But before he committed suicide, he received the news that the Senate proclaimed him as an enemy of the state and planned to humiliate him with a public beating and an execution. However, this news was untrue. The Senate wanted to get rid of Nero, but it did not decide on any acts yet. They had served the imperial Julio-Claudian family for so long that they wanted to make peace with its only representative until he at least produced an heir. However, the emperor lost his nerve and ordered one of his companions to kill him. Thus, Nero became the first Roman emperor to commit suicide, even though it was assisted. Emperor Nero died on June 9th, 68, ending the Julio-Claudian dynasty. Only then did the Senate proclaim him as a public enemy, and the senators welcomed Galba as the new emperor. They did this out of fear of Galba, who was the first out of four emperors to rule in the year 69.

The Flavian Dynasty

On January 1st, 69, the legions stationed in upper Germany revolted against Galba's rule and proclaimed Aulus Vitellius as their emperor. He was the son of a famous military commander who served the Julio-Claudian dynasty his whole life. Although Aulus had no military or public experience, his father's fame was enough to secure him military support. Galba entered Rome and was declared the emperor by the Senate, but he quickly managed to estrange everyone. He refused to pay the military what he had promised them for their support, and the army largely abandoned him. The Praetorian Guard swore their allegiance to the empire but only in the Senate's name, refusing to mention Galba. The new emperor also managed to inspire hatred in the citizens of Rome by killing around 7,000 men he considered to be loyal to Nero. There were no trials or proper accusations, only massacres.

The last mistake Galba made was to name Lucius Calpurnius Piso as his successor instead of Marcus Salvius Otho, who had served him faithfully. In retaliation, Otho bribed and persuaded the Praetorian Guard to support him. Within just a few days, Galba and Piso were assassinated. The Senate and the Romans declared Otho their new emperor on January 15th, 69. However, the troops stationed in the Roman province were not satisfied with this decision. The legions that supported Aulus Vitellius as their emperor slowly marched to Rome. Otho didn't want a civil war, so he sent emissaries to negotiate peace. However, the commanders of Vitellius's army wouldn't hear about Otho's proposals; they wanted war. The bloody clash of the two armies occurred in April in two separate battles, where more than 40,000 men lost their lives on both sides. The decisive Battle of Bedriacum showed Otho how powerful his enemy was, and rather than prolonging the civil war, the new emperor decided to commit suicide. Vitellius entered Rome, but he had no support from the Praetorian Guard. He also proved incapable of making any state decisions, which instigated further unrest.

In July, the troops in Judea proclaimed their commander, Titus Flavius Vespasianus (Vespasian), as their emperor. This trend quickly spread to the troops in Syria, Egypt, and other provinces in Africa, who also gave their support to Vespasian. Since Egypt was an extremely important province, as it controlled the supply of grain to Rome, Vespasian's position was very good. The threat of famine was serious, and the army of Italy started taking Vespasian's side. But it wasn't only the famine that changed their minds. Vitellius proved to be more interested in spending imperial money on lavish dinner parties instead of leading the Roman Empire. He was a bad choice as an emperor, and he quickly lost the little military support he had.

The troops of Pannonia were the first to react and started marching to Rome. The clash with Vitellius's army occurred in October at the city of Cremona, where the Pannonian legion was victorious. They continued their march, and in December, they stormed the city. Vitellius was killed, and the fighting on the streets of Rome was so fierce that it destroyed almost half the city. The Senate and the people were forced to declare Vespasian as the new emperor, the fourth one in that year. However, the new emperor took his time on his way to Rome. He arrived in the city in October of the next year (70 CE). However, once in power, Vespasian proved himself capable of restoring peace to the Roman Empire. He ruled for ten years and founded the Flavian dynasty.

Vespasian (r. 69–79 CE)

Bust of Emperor Vespasian
Originally uploaded by user:shakko, CC BY-SA 3.0
<*https://creativecommons.org/licenses/by-sa/3.0*>, *via Wikimedia Commons*
https://commons.wikimedia.org/wiki/File:Vespasianus01_pushkin_edit.png

Vespasian was a famous military leader, and it was the military support that brought him to the head of the Roman Empire. However, his skills as a civil leader were unknown, and he had to quickly employ them. When he took the throne, Vespasian had to deal with the ongoing Jewish revolt. He left Judea in the hands of his eldest son, Titus, and ordered him to storm Jerusalem. Titus did so and even destroyed the Jewish temple and its Holy of Holies (a Jewish term to mark the part of the temple where God appears). A series of regulations for Jews were brought into effect. They were not allowed to spread their religion, and only those who were born Jews were allowed to practice it. The temple taxes collected around Judea were used for the renovation of the temple of Jupiter

Optimus Maximus in Rome, which had been destroyed during the civil war in which Vespasian became emperor. Jews were also not allowed to celebrate Roman holidays but were exempted from participating in the imperial cult. The fall of Jerusalem was the end of the Jewish revolt, even though the guerilla fighting continued for the next three years.

Vespasian used the victory over Judea to advertise himself and his family as the bringers of peace to the Roman Empire. To celebrate the victory over the Jews, Vespasian built the Temple of Peace in central Rome. Near that, he started building an amphitheater, which is today known as the Colosseum. Both constructions were built by Jewish slaves, and the booty from the war with Judea was used to pay for the buildings.

Other areas rose in revolt too. In Germany, the people saw an opportunity to gain their independence. Soon, they were joined by the Gauls, who continued with occasional unrest even after the rebellion was quelled. The constant insurgencies, which occurred in the areas alongside the Germanic border, lasted until 96 CE and the end of Domitian's rule (81-96). Vespasian also reinforced the eastern border of the empire by sending troops to Syria. Parthia was a constant threat there, but no major conflict broke out. The east saw many new roads being built by the Flavian dynasty, as Rome needed quicker means of transportation for the new troops. In 72, Vespasian added Commagene to the province of Syria, and he garrisoned Cappadocia, which also gained some territories of Lesser Armenia.

Not much is known about Vespasian's government outside of the war. He did grant 350 cities of the Iberian Peninsula the status of Latin cities. The citizens of these cities automatically gained Roman citizenship and the rights that came with it. The local laws and procedures were now strongly influenced by the Romans, but officially, the cities could retain whatever local self-governing models they had developed throughout the centuries. The citizenship given to the people of the Iberian Peninsula meant they were now legally allowed to climb the social ladder of Rome and to enter the civil service.

The years 73 and 74 saw a series of new tax regulations, in which some of the tax exemptions implemented by previous emperors were now abolished. The state was in a financial crisis because of the revolts in Judea and Germany, as well as because of the many building projects Vespasian undertook. To recover the treasury, Vespasian led a completely different life than his predecessor Nero. He didn't like to indulge in luxurious parties, and he never bought expensive presents for his guests. Instead, he implemented a soundly based collection of taxes throughout the empire, and he committed to the restitution of public land to communities. Because Vespasian refrained from increasing taxes as much as he could, he was highly praised by his contemporaries as the emperor who managed to save the country from financial disaster without putting new burdens on its people. Taxes were raised, although the people barely felt the increase, as Vespasian didn't collect them as capriciously as Nero.

Vespasian was a modest emperor who worked hard, together with the Senate, to improve the state. He even continued Claudius's expansion of the empire into the territory of Britain. In 78, Vespasian sent his generals to conquer the northern parts of Britain, and they succeeded in acquiring some of the territories that today belong to Scotland. Vespasian also introduced a form of censorship to Rome. Many Stoic and Cynic philosophers were expelled from the city for their teachings. They were joined by astrologers and writers who opposed the emperor's rule. On the other hand, historians and writers who praised Vespasian and his Flavian dynasty were greatly rewarded. But Vespasian's rule wasn't long, as he died of illness in 79.

Vespasian was succeeded by his eldest son, Titus, who ruled for only two years. Titus didn't have time to prove himself as the emperor of Rome because he died from a fever in 81. However, the Senate deified him for his efforts in relieving two major disasters that happened in Rome. The first was the eruption of Mount Vesuvius in 79, and the second was the great fire of Rome in 80. Titus was more than capable of dealing with these disasters, and he worked very hard to mitigate losses. His actions only confirmed the people's love for him, as he didn't come to power unprepared. He served as a consul seven times, one year as a censor, and even became the praetorian prefect before his father's death. Unfortunately, Titus died prematurely, and he left no male heir behind him. Rome was handed to his younger brother, Domitian.

Domitian (r. 81–96)

Bust of Emperor Domitian
I, Sailko, CC BY-SA 3.0 <http://creativecommons.org/licenses/by-sa/3.0/>, via Wikimedia Commons https://commons.wikimedia.org/wiki/File:Domiziano_da_collezione_albani,_fine_del_I_sec._dc._02.J PG

After the death of Emperor Titus, his younger brother Domitian was elevated to the position, with the support of the Praetorian Guard. However, this young emperor wasn't prepared for such a role. Unfortunately, he was largely ignored by his father and his brother, as he was never really seen as an option for the succession.

His previous roles in the politics of Rome were largely ceremonial, and he never held any executive power. Because of this, he never developed a strong reliance on the Senate, and during his rule, he was seen as an autocrat. This is true to some extent, but he was also the most efficient emperor since Claudius, as he effectively stabilized the economic and social aspects of the Roman Empire. The Senate was constantly against him because he took away some of their powers, but Domitian had the love of the people and the army. This proved enough for him to rule for fifteen years, which was the longest rule in Roman history since Tiberius.

It wasn't enough for Domitian to be proclaimed the princeps; he also held consulship every year from 82 to 88. In 84/85, he became the perpetual censor, taking away the senators' ability to rise to that office. Domitian was known for accumulating various offices for himself and leaving the Senate with little executive power. This divided him from the people of high social circles, and contemporary writers liked to represent him as a ruthless and paranoid autocrat. Supposedly, he committed atrocities while trying to censor public morale. He meddled in religion too. He accused many Vestal Virgins of immorality. After a brief trial, they were put to death, and one of the Vestal Virgins was even buried alive as punishment. There is even a story about how Domitian seduced his niece Julia, Titus's daughter. Once she became pregnant, he forced her to have an abortion, and she died in the process.

Despite this, Domitian continued to be popular among the people and soldiers. He started many building projects, which secured work for the commoners. He also invested in various games to the delight of the people. For the army, he increased their annual salary by one-third of what they had previously received. Beginning in 83, Domitian himself embarked on campaigns, for which the army praised him. In Germany, across the Rhine, the emperor pacified the rebels with such decisive victories that he earned the title Germanicus. In military endeavors, Domitian is probably best known for fighting the Dacians, even though he never really managed to defeat their king, Decebalus. When Decebalus crossed the Danube in 84 and entered the territory of the Roman province of Moesia, Domitian went personally to deal with the problem. The Roman emperor even planned an invasion on Dacian territory and was successful until he reached the capital of Sarmizegetusa. Unfortunately, another war broke out in Germany, and not wanting to fight on two fronts, Domitian struck a deal with Decebalus. He would pay the Dacians eight million sesterces a year for the right to transport Roman troops through Dacian territory.

Back in Rome, Domitian's personality worsened. He became paranoid and placed mirrors throughout his residency so he could see if anyone was about to attack him from behind. He also demanded to be called *Dominus et Deus* ("Lord and God"), and he often accused people of atheism, even the members of his own family. He built a cult of personality around himself and expected to be worshiped. Soon, the people who used to love him became indifferent toward him, and it is said that Romans didn't even react when they heard the news of his death. Domitian died in 96 CE. He was assassinated by the conspirators in his court.

The Five Good Emperors and the Nerva-Antonine Dynasty

The term "Five Good Emperors" comes from an Italian diplomat named Niccolò Machiavelli. In his work, the *Discourses on Livy*, he argues that Nerva, Trajan, Hadrian, Antoninus Pius, and Marcus Aurelius were the Five Good Emperors and that all of their predecessors and successors (except Titus) were bad for the politics of ancient Rome. Machiavelli argues that all the bad emperors inherited the throne by birth, while these five were all adopted. They had to do much more than simply be the heir of Rome. They had to prove their worth through their political careers and military achievements. This work gave them the basis on which they ruled. The term "Five Good Emperors" is still used in history to mark the reign of these Roman emperors.

Domitian's death marked a new era in the history of Rome. Many 18th-century scholars called this period, which lasted for the next 180 years, as the era of prosperity for the human race. The next imperial dynasty of Rome would bring about a new administration that was linked with prosperity and peace. Child support for the lowborn was established, the urbanization of provinces was encouraged, and the judicial system was standardized throughout the whole empire. During this period, religious tolerance was at its peak, and the Roman expansionist wars were quick and successful.

But was it all so perfect during the reign of the Nerva-Antonine dynasty? The scholars of the 18th century had many texts from the contemporary writers at their disposal, and they based their opinions on texts written by the emperors' supporters. Modern scholars have revealed this was an era where censorship was strong, as every speech against the ruler was harshly punished. Emperors had to use propaganda to receive the people's support, and any political opposition was punishable. In these circumstances, it is hard to make a difference between the truth and propaganda. Modern archaeology revealed that common people left little to no trail in history during these times, which makes us wonder what their life was like. Were they really satisfied with the situation in the empire? Why didn't they leave anything behind? The only possible answer was that their lives were so destitute that they simply had nothing to leave.

Nerva (r. 96-98)

Bronze statue of Emperor Nerva in Rome
Steerpike, CC BY-SA 3.0 <https://creativecommons.org/licenses/by-sa/3.0>, via Wikimedia Commons https://commons.wikimedia.org/wiki/File:Nerva_Forum_Romanum.png

Marcus Cocceius Nerva used to be one of the counselors to the previous emperor, Domitian, but he took no part in the assassination plot. Instead, he was chosen by the senators as the next emperor. This was a very odd choice. It was not because he was a supporter of Domitian, but because he was already a very old man who had no children. But perhaps it was his seniority that pleased the Senate. He lacked military experience, but he served as a consul and had some distinctions in civic service. Also, he was one of the rare politicians who survived both the Julio-Claudian and Flavian dynasties. To make sure of their safety, the Senate made him swear that he would not kill any of their members.

Only two years into his reign, Nerva managed to implement some of the most successful changes to Roman society. He gave around sixty million sesterces to help poor Romans who had no land of their own. But he left the land acquisition and assignment of lots to the Senate, showing his trust in them. He also implemented the *alimenta*, from which today's child alimony is derived. The Roman *alimenta* was a loan to the Italian landowners, who agreed to pay a 5 percent interest tax, which would be given to the families in need of child support. He also abolished the tax Jews had to pay for practicing their religion (which had been implemented by Vespasian), and many provinces were granted special tax conditions and even exemptions.

Because Nerva never distinguished himself in the military, he lacked the support of the army and the Praetorian Guard. He further agitated the army by not allowing them to pursue Domitian's assassins. Eventually, he agreed, but this wasn't enough to appease the soldiers. It was only when childless Nerva adopted Marcus Ulpius Trajanus (Trajan) as his son and heir and secured him a consulship in 98 that the tensions between him and the military stopped. Trajan was born and raised in the Roman province of Spain, and as such, he was the first emperor born outside of Rome. Nerva was aware of Trajan's military successes and predicted he would be a good choice as emperor. Because Trajan was loved by the army, the power would smoothly transfer from Nerva to him.

Nerva died on January 28th, 96, due to a stroke and fever. Even though his rule was short, he did so much for the people of Rome that the Senate decided to deify him.

Trajan (r. 98–117)

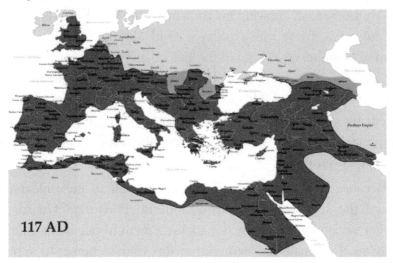

The Roman Empire under Emperor Trajan

Tataryn, CC BY-SA 3.0 <https://creativecommons.org/licenses/by-sa/3.0>, via Wikimedia Commons https://commons.wikimedia.org/wiki/File:Roman_Empire_Trajan_117AD.png

Even though the Senate proclaimed Trajan as the emperor of Rome, he chose to stay in the provinces, securing their borders. The first time he entered Rome was in 99 CE, and he did so on foot, wearing civilian robes. Perhaps he did this to show his modesty and unwillingness to rule, which pleased the Senate, or he did it to show how he was nothing more than just one of the Roman citizens. Either way, his entrance was effective because he managed to win over the masses and rule peacefully in conjunction with the Senate.

Trajan proved to be an effective emperor. He involved himself in many civilian matters, yet he never forgot that he came from the military ranks. He started many building projects to improve the empire and military conquests to expand it. Therefore, he is remembered as one of the most capable emperor-generals. Even the Senate honored him by proclaiming him *Optimus Princeps*— "Best Ruler." He is still remembered as one of the best emperors Rome ever had. He was a philanthropist, a builder, military commander, and social revolutionist. During his reign, the Roman Empire achieved its maximum territorial extent.

Even though Trajan gave the impression he wanted to share his rule with the Senate, in reality, he was the one holding the ultimate power. It turns out the speech he gave in 100 CE, where he asked the Senate to help him rule, was nothing more than an act. His political opponents remembered him as an individual who made all the decisions. All state functions depended on him, and no member of the Senate was to exercise their executive powers without Trajan's approval. Trajan was lucky his opinion often matched that of the Senate; therefore, there was no real conflict between the two. Even though Trajan showed all the signs of an autocrat, he was still considered a good ruler because he made an example of himself. He ruled with virtue and morals instead of with fear and state intrigues.

Trajan's fame to this day comes from his war with Dacia (territory of today's Romania and Moldova, including smaller parts of Serbia, Bulgaria, Ukraine, Poland, Slovakia, and Hungary). During these times, Dacia was an organized kingdom, capable of making alliances and posing a real threat to Rome. The other European provinces of Rome were mostly unorganized tribal states that were easy to conquer. Dacia showed its strength when its king, Decebalus, forced Dominican to sign an unfavorable treaty. Aside from this, Dacia was a strategically important land and rich with natural gold, silver, and iron mines. It was a perfect target for Trajan, as its lands would greatly benefit Rome.

The first attack on Dacia was launched in May 101. Dacia proved to be a much stronger enemy than what Trajan had anticipated, and it took two separate wars to bring it down. The first war was fought between 101 and 102, while the second lasted from 105 to 106. The first defeat the Dacians experienced was on the shores of the Danube, in a region known as the Iron Gates of Transylvania. There, Trajan built a road and a bridge so his troops could cross the river for future attacks on Dacia. Today, the road is flooded, but Tabula Trajana, a monument to the emperor, remains.

A modern sculptor carved the head of King Decebalus into the cliffs overlooking the Danube in the 1990s so the king of old could watch the ancient road and the coming of his enemies.

The colossal head of Decebalus on the Danube between Serbia and Romania
Yanko Malinov, CC BY-SA 4.0 <https://creativecommons.org/licenses/by-sa/4.0>,
via Wikimedia Commons
https://commons.wikimedia.org/wiki/File:Frontal_view_of_the_Decebalus_rock_sculpture.jpg

But the defeat at the Iron Gates didn't mean Dacia was conquered. The Roman casualties were so high that Trajan had to retreat and gather more forces. In the meantime, Decebalus launched a counterattack but was defeated when Trajan came with the reinforcements from Rome. The next year, the Dacians submitted when the Romans entered deep into their territory. King Decebalus committed suicide by slitting his own throat to avoid being captured and humiliated in Rome. Nevertheless, his head was taken to Rome, where it was thrown down the stairs of Trajan's newly built forum.

After the defeat of Decebalus, Dacia was made a client kingdom, and later on, it was even annexed by Rome. The spoils of war were tremendous, and legend has it that after the first war, Trajan brought two tons of pure gold back to Rome. There is no way of knowing how much Rome profited from its victory over Dacia, but the acquired wealth from these two wars financed new building works not only in the city of Rome but throughout the whole empire. Trajan celebrated his victory over Dacia by ordering 123 days of games to be held for three years. Unfortunately, the Romans destroyed much of the Dacian culture, and little is known today about these people, who were capable of threatening the great Roman Empire. Trajan also brought migrants from all over the empire to settle in newly conquered territories, mostly Celtic tribes from northern provinces. The Romanization of the Dacian territory was extremely successful, and the Dacians quickly adopted the Latin language, culture, and religion. In fact, to this day, Romanian is one of the few surviving Latin languages that are close to the original Latin of imperial Rome.

The success against Dacia probably inspired Trajan to expand his empire even more. In 106, he annexed Nabataea (Jordan), at the time known as part of Arabia Petraea. This area was of particular importance, as it was a trade route to India. It was also rich in spices, incense, and precious stones. New problems arose in 110 when the Roman vassal king of Armenia died and was replaced by the Parthian king. The war with Parthia would keep Trajan occupied until his death in 117 CE. During the Parthian war, Trajan annexed Armenia, Assyria, and Mesopotamia. The emperor left his protege Hadrian to deal with the war in the east while he started the journey back to Rome, as he was ill. On his way home, Trajan allegedly adopted Hadrian officially, making him his heir. The journey was long, and Trajan suffered from his illness throughout the spring and summer of 117, which was when he finally died, never reaching his destination.

Hadrian (r. 117-138)

Hadrian's Wall, forming the Roman border in northern England

Just like his predecessor, Hadrian was from Spain. Perhaps this was the reason why Trajan took young Hadrian under his protection. He also married his protege to his grand-niece, but this marriage never produced a child. Hadrian was supported by the Senate and the military, as he was a very successful military commander. But he managed to estrange the Senate, as he ordered the execution of four senators during the first year of his rule. The reasons for the executions are unknown today, but it seems the Senate never forgave him. Another reason why Hadrian wasn't popular was that his imperial ideals were very different from those of his predecessors. Instead of expanding the empire, Hadrian wanted it to be consolidated. He wanted strong borders that would fluctuate over time and could be easily defended. Hadrian's Wall, the northern limit of the Roman Empire in Britannia, is one such example of what he had in mind. Hadrian spent most of his time visiting the borders of the empire, and he was the only Roman emperor who visited almost all of its provinces.

Hadrian ruled for twenty-one years, and he spent most of the time improving the Roman Empire from within. He improved the administration and various infrastructure, most notably the communications between the provinces. He invigorated religious practices by raising new temples around the empire (especially in Athens). Hadrian was a lover of arts and culture, and he wanted the Roman Empire to be seen as the world's cultural center. But his favorite city was Athens, and he devoted himself to reviving its artistic scene. The third of the "Five Good Emperors" was an artist himself. He was known for designing the buildings, and he also painted and wrote poetry. He wrote his own speeches, and in time, he wrote an autobiography.

During Hadrian's rule, the Third Jewish Revolt, known as the Bar Kokhba revolt, occurred (123–135). This conflict is known as one of the most devastating wars in Judea, in which 50 Jewish outposts and 985 villages were destroyed (according to Cassius Dio, a contemporary historian). After the revolt, Hadrian renamed Judea to Syria Palaestina. He rebuilt Jerusalem in the Greek style and banned Jews from entering the city. At this point, Romans started differentiating between Christians and Jews more clearly.

One of the many accomplishments of Hadrian was to set the rule over the Roman Empire for the next two generations. He had no natural children, but he adopted Titus Aurelius Fulvus Boionius Arrius Antoninus (Antoninus Pius) in 138 and ordered him to adopt two young boys who would be his heirs. Those boys were seventeen-year-old Marcus Arrius Antoninus, better known as Marcus Aurelius, and seven-year-old Lucius Verus, who would later join Marcus Aurelius in ruling over the empire. All three choices for Hadrian's heirs were of Spanish and Gallic descent, but they were also members of wealthy families. The Roman custom of adoption allowed them to be lifted to the position of princeps. By appointing his heirs for the next two generations, Hadrian secured stability for Rome. He died on July 10th, 138 CE.

Antoninus Pius (r. 138–161)

Bust of Emperor Antoninus Pius
https://commons.wikimedia.org/wiki/File:Antoninus_Pius_Glyptothek_Munich_337_cropped.jpg

After Hadrian's death, his heir Antoninus earned the nickname Pius (pious) because of his success in convincing the Senate to deify his predecessor. His rule was calm and prosperous. Antoninus never left Italy and was remembered for leaving the empire with a well-off treasury. This was due to his effective administration and his uninterest in luxurious parties. The Roman Empire did not conquer new lands during his rule, as he continued Hadrian's policy of reinforcing the empire's existing borders. The only military success known to be from this time was the reconquest of southern Scotland, where the Antonine Wall was built.

The rule of Antoninus Pius seems uneventful, and a reader might get the impression that he was the weakest of the Roman emperors. But this couldn't be further from the truth. He, too, belongs to the "Five Good Emperors" club because he succeeded in keeping the peace in the vast Roman Empire. The uneventfulness of his rule speaks of his ability to hold the empire together. Many scholars consider this period to be the climax of the Roman Empire, as everything was in perfect order. Of course, minor skirmishes on the outer borders of the empire occurred, but Antoninus was quick to quell any rebellions and to pacify unrestful regions.

The fact that the first Roman mission to China was sent around this time speaks further how prosperous and peaceful Rome was. The texts discovered in the *Book of the Later Han* speaks about the Roman embassy arriving in Han China in 166. The journey might have taken the Romans several years, considering it was the mid-2nd century. Their arrival would also have been slowed down by the various exotic countries the ambassadors encountered on their way. Nevertheless, the date of 166 makes it impossible to conclude whether the mission to China was sent during the reign of Antoninus or his successor, Marcus Aurelius.

Marcus Aurelius (r. 161–180)

Bust of Emperor Marcus Aurelius
Musée Saint-Raymond, CC BY-SA 4.0 <https://creativecommons.org/licenses/by-sa/4.0>, via Wikimedia Commons https://commons.wikimedia.org/wiki/File:MSR-ra-61-b-1-DM.jpg

Marcus Aurelius was the last of the "Five Good Emperors," and he was the last ruler of the *Pax Romana*. He smoothly took over the imperium, just as Hadrian had arranged in 138. But he didn't rule alone. He was joined by his adoptive brother Lucius Verus (r. 161–169), who married Aurelius's daughter Lucilla. She was only fourteen, while her husband was thirty-four years old. The Mediterranean world practiced marriage in this way, in which females would marry at a young age while the males were in late adulthood. This ensured high fertility rates to keep up with the enormous mortality rates of the population. But it was also seen as culturally appropriate. The role of a woman was to give birth and care for the children, while men were expected to prove themselves in civic or military service before starting a family.

After the death of Antoninus, the Senate was prepared to install Marcus Aurelius as the sole ruler, but he refused the office unless his adoptive brother was given equal power. They ruled together, albeit with some challenges, for the next eight years. However, the Senate soon proclaimed Marcus the pontifex maximus (chief high priest), and with this title, he became the senior emperor. It was clear that Aurelius was the one with greater authority. The two emperors were successful in quelling the unrests that rose in Britain and Germany at the beginning of their rule. Most of the time, the two emperors were away from each other. While Marcus ruled in Rome and led the forces of the northern frontiers, Verus was stationed in the east, where he commanded the army fighting against Parthia (162–166).

At the end of the Parthian war, the soldiers who had fought in the east brought a terrible disease known as the Antonine Plague back to Rome. Today, it is believed the outbreak wasn't a plague at all but a smallpox epidemic. After 166, the epidemic spread throughout the Roman Empire, where it continued to ravage the land for the next twenty-five years. The military camps were hit the hardest, but the civilians in the cities suffered too. It is estimated the epidemic took the lives of more than a fifth of the citizens in Alexandria. When the disease spread to the rural areas, famines followed, as there were not enough people to produce food. Rome was spared, though, and life in the city continued as it had. Monuments were built, art was produced, and architecture flourished. All of this gave the impression that the elite members of society continued to lead comfortable urbane lives.

When the war with Parthia ended in 166, trouble began to brew north of the empire. The two emperors had decided to pull a number of legions from Germany so they could reinforce the border with Parthia. The Germanic tribes saw this as an opportunity to cross the Danube and invade the areas of Pannonia and Dacia. In 168, Aurelius and Verus traveled north to defend their territories. The next year, Verus suddenly died of a stroke, leaving Marcus Aurelius as the sole ruler of the Roman Empire. For the rest of his life, Aurelius spent most of his time in the north, fending off the invading Germanic tribes. He detested warfare, as his Stoic philosophy taught him that war was the opposite of goodness, to which people should strive. However, he understood the Roman Empire was his duty, and as a Stoic, he had to overcome his personal feelings and continue doing what was best for Rome. The war in the north was divided into two major conflicts, which are known as the First and Second Marcomannic Wars (166–173 and 176–180, respectively). During these wars, Roman authority extended across the Danube, and two new provinces were added to the empire: Marcomannia and Sarmatia.

The only sign of internal unrest in the Roman Empire during the rule of Marcus Aurelius was in 175, when the governor of Egypt, Avidius Cassius, declared the emperor dead and himself the emperor in the east. It is uncertain if he actually received fake news of Aurelius's death or if he fabricated it himself. Nevertheless, he ruled for almost four months before he was assassinated. Marcus Aurelius was on his way to deal with the problem in the east, but he didn't even reach his destination before his authority there was restored. But the fact that Cassius so easily took over a part of the empire only shed light on the empire's underlying divisions. The territories of the Roman Empire became so vast that proper communication was impossible. Without communication, maintaining political unity was impossible.

Marcus Aurelius died of natural causes in 180, and his nineteen-year-old son, Commodus, became the sole emperor of Rome. He had ruled alongside his father since 176, which was when the Senate gave him the title of Augustus. Although he was young and inexperienced, Commodus had the best tutors his father could arrange for him. He was constantly surrounded by philosophers and military experts who could teach him, but it is unknown if he ever fought in a war personally before becoming the emperor. Unlike his father, Commodus is remembered for being a megalomaniac and a dictator. His rule is considered to be the end of Rome's golden age of peace. Although there were no major wars fought during his reign, Commodus started a series of scandals and intrigues that would lead to the empire's downfall. He ruled from 176 until 192, the year he was assassinated. He was declared a public enemy posthumously.

Chapter 6 – The Third and Early Fourth Centuries

After the assassination of Commodus, different groups of politicians sued for power. Everyone had a candidate of their own, including the Senate, the Praetorian Guard, and the army. The army had three different candidates for the emperor, depending on which division they belonged to. During the first year after the fall of Commodus, five different emperors were on the throne. Then one showed up, one who was able to maintain and expand his control. His name was Septimius Severus (r. 193–211), and he was promoted by the troops stationed along the Danube. Septimius entered Rome dressed in a civilian toga, just like Trajan did in his days. However, unlike Trajan, he allowed his cavalry and infantry forces to follow him. This way, he showed the people he was one of them but one with an army behind him to back him up.

Once Septimius Severus grasped power in Rome, the first thing he had to do was deal with his opponents. He chased his enemy, Gaius Pescennius Niger, an imperial legate to Syria who briefly ruled the empire before Septimius. Septimius killed Niger in 194 CE and restarted the war with Parthia, claiming they had protected his enemy. In 196, Septimius had himself posthumously adopted into the family of Marcus Aurelius, and the Senate approved. This gave him a connection with the last of the "Good Emperors," which granted him the legitimacy to rule Rome. Soon, he elevated his eleven-year-old son to the position of co-ruler by giving him the title Augustus. He also renamed him Marcus Aurelius Antoninus, but the boy and the future emperor of Rome remained known by his nickname, "Caracalla," which is derived from the name for a Gallic hooded tunic.

Septimius Severus remained loved by the army because he fought alongside the soldiers and shared their hardship during the long campaigns in distant lands. In 211, he died in Britain. During the rule of Septimius Severus, the army was greatly reformed, and it became a way of life for many families. Soldiers were now allowed to marry and have families while serving the army. This had been banned during the reign of Augustus, and with this switch in policy came the family tradition of soldiering. Young sons were recruited by their fathers, and the numbers of legions swelled up.

Caracalla joined his father's rule in 198, but from 211 until 217, he was the sole ruler of the Roman Empire. He was quite different from his father. He had no charisma and often ruled with pure brutality. In 212, he gave Roman citizenship to all the people who lived within the borders of the empire. However, his intentions were not to improve the people's rights. Only Roman citizens were eligible to pay the 5 percent inheritance tax, and the emperor lacked money. To gather some, he imposed this tax on everyone, even those who couldn't pay it. In 213 and 214, the Roman Empire's borders were constantly under attack, and Caracalla needed the army's goodwill to fight off the attackers. To please the soldiers, he raised their annual salaries from 2,000 sesterces to 3,000. This only drained the imperial treasury more, and the tactic of raising more taxes by giving everyone citizenship ultimately failed. In 217, Caracalla was stabbed by a soldier, who had been egged on by Caracalla's successor, Marcus Opellius Macrinus (r. 217-218).

Macrinus only ruled for one year. Even though he started with the support of the army, he soon lost it. First, he angered his troops by cowardly making peace with the Parthians. After that, he cut back the soldiers' salaries, which was enough for the army to give their support to fourteen-year-old Varius Avitus Bassianus, who was allegedly the son of the deceased Caracalla. The soldiers killed Macrinus and saluted the young boy as their new emperor. Bassianus took the name Marcus Aurelius Antoninus, but he remained known as Emperor Elagabalus, which was the name of the Syrian sun god. He ruled for only four years, from 218 until 222, and it was one of the strangest periods in the history of the Roman Empire. Elagabalus tried to force his religion of the sun god, which was represented in the form of black stone, on Rome. The religious rituals belonging to this deity were filled with orgies and unusual sexual demands. To unite this new religion with the Roman one, the teenage emperor married a Vestal Virgin, which was sacrilege of the old Roman traditions. Elagabalus was killed by the Praetorian Guard, which was bribed by his cousins to install Marcus Aurelius Severus Alexander on the throne. He was the son of Elagabalus's aunt, Julia Mamaea.

Severus Alexander was also only fourteen years old when he rose to power in 222, and he ruled for the next thirteen years. However, his mother's titles of "Mother of Augustus, and the Camps, and of the Senate, and the fatherland" suggest that she was the one making all the decisions. However, Severus Alexander was despised by the army, and his rule was marked by many military uprisings in Rome. In 232, Severus Alexander successfully campaigned in Antioch, but he was unable to defeat the German invaders in Raetia in 235 (parts of today's Switzerland, Germany, and Austria). When he began to negotiate with the Germanic tribes, his soldiers saw it as a sign of weakness. As a result, the emperor and his mother were killed by the soldiers. The next period of Roman history saw a series of "soldier-emperors," of whom first was Gaius Julius Verus Maximus. The 3rd century and the beginning of the 4th century were turbulent times, in which the Roman Empire suffered pressures from outside of their borders and started crumbling.

One of the most significant "soldier-emperors" was Lucius Domitius Aurelianus (better known as Aurelian), who ruled from 270 until 275 CE. He was an Illyrian commander, and he became the emperor after the approval of his troops. His rule was marked by military campaigns, and he was nicknamed "Hand-on-Sword" because of his readiness to fight various invaders anywhere in the empire. The first to feel his wrath were the northerners, who managed to enter the Romans' territory in Italy. But soon, he had to turn to the east, where he defeated Zenobia of Palmyra (the queen of an empire that arose in the territory of today's Syria) in two separate campaigns. But Aurelian wasn't always so successful in administering the Roman provinces. He decided to completely abandon Dacia and removed all Roman forces stationed there because he believed this territory was no longer defendable from outsiders. He is also known for building the walls around Rome, beginning in 271. Although this practice wasn't unusual for the cities of the Roman provinces, the Aurelian Walls were the tallest and thickest defenses the city ever had.

Diocletian and the Tetrarchy

The Roman Empire under the Tetrarchy

When Aurelian was killed in 275, ten more years of political instability occurred. There were many military conflicts, and various political enemies were at each other's throat. But the time of political and military tensions ended in 284 with the rise of Gaius Aurelius Valerius Diocletianus, better known as Diocletian. He would become the first emperor to hold power for more than a few years, as six unable emperors came before Diocletian's rule. He was also the first Roman emperor to willingly abdicate.

Diocletian is an oddity among the Roman emperors. He had no higher education, no excessive military training, and no previous senatorial experience. He wasn't a part of the Roman elite, as he came from a modest Dalmatian family. However, he was widely accepted because of his empirical mind and willingness to implement methodical changes throughout the empire. He ruled for twenty-one years, from 284 until 305, during which time he brought many reforms to the light of day. Among them was the famous Tetrarchy, the rule of four. However, this new rule was much more than four emperors sharing equal power. The system was more complicated, as it had two senior emperors with the titles Caesar and two younger ones who could be vetoed at any time by their co-rulers.

Diocletian also revised the empire's administration, and he also brought back the loyalty of the armies and their effectiveness. If it wasn't for his reforms, the Roman Empire would have crumbled much sooner. Probably the most important reform Diocletian made was when it came to the rule. Diocletian changed it from the Principate (where the emperor was the first among equals), which had been established by Augustus, to the Dominate, the absolute rule of a *dominus* (master). With Diocletian, the empire was established with the meaning we prescribe to the word today. The *dominus* was the emperor, a person elevated above his subjects and approachable only by the select few. The administrative and court officials were the ones to have contact with the people, not the emperor himself. In the year 300, Diocletian took away all the powers of the Senate, rendering it useless. However, the Senate continued to exist, and its tasks were now to oversee the public games and try minor offenders. But the Senate couldn't act alone. Everything needed the emperor's approval.

When Diocletian first came to the throne, the empire was in a state of continuous rebellions. Various provinces organized small uprisings, and each had to be dealt with, from the bagaudae (peasants or bandits) in Gaul to the native tribes of Asia Minor. Aside from rebellions, the empire was threatened by invasions from outside its borders. The Franks, Alamanni, and Goths from the lower Rhine and Danube regularly made incursions into Roman territories. To the east and south, the Sassanids, Berbers, and other nomadic tribes of Africa entered Mauritania and Spain across the Strait of Gibraltar. Diocletian sent his friend Marcus Aurelius Valerius Maximianus, better known as Maximian, to deal with the incursions in the north. For his success, he was raised to the position of co-ruler, or Augustus, in 286. But when Britain rebelled in 287, the two emperors were unable to make headway. The new Gothic incursions made them abandon the case of Britain, for the time being. Pressed from all sides, the two rulers realized they needed help to save their territory.

In 293, the Tetrarchy was organized when Diocletian divided the Roman world between the famous military commanders who were tied to him through marriages. Diocletian remained the ruler above all, and he gained the title *Jovius* (Jupiter-like). He was the Augustus of the East, with the capital in Nicomedia (Izmir in Turkey). Gaius Galerius Valerius Maximianus (better known as Galerius) was the next in line, the one who would succeed Diocletian. He ruled the southern parts of the empire and had two capitals, one in Sirmium (Sremska Mitrovica, Serbia) and Thessalonica (Thessaloniki, Greece). In the West, the previously proclaimed Augustus Maximian ruled. His capital was in Mediolanum (Milan, Italy), and he remained the second most powerful person in the Roman Empire. His Caesar was Marcus Flavius Valerius Constantius (better known as simply Constantius), the father of the future emperor Constantine the Great. His capital was in Augusta Treverorum (Trier, Germany) near the German border, and his territories were in the north. All four rulers were constantly on the move, and they rarely gathered in the same place. They also very rarely visited the capital of the whole empire, Rome itself.

The Tetrarchy proved to be effective in dealing with the rebellions and small-scale invasions. In 298, the unrest was subdued in Egypt by Diocletian, while Galerius defeated the Sassanids in Mesopotamia. Maximian recovered Mauretania from the Berbers of Africa, while Constantius kept peace in Britannia and the upper Rhine region. In 303, they celebrated Diocletian's and Maximian's twentieth anniversary of their rule in Rome.

By the year 303, the Roman Empire had 101 provinces, which were within twelve (later fifteen) larger units named *dioecesis*. Each of the larger units was administered by a *vicarius*, a deputy, who, in turn, answered to the praetorian prefects. But instead of being the head of the imperial guard, the praetorian prefects were now the chief administrators of the four rulers. Provincial governors still existed, but their role was reduced to collecting taxes and administering justice.

During Diocletian's Tetrarchy, the harassment of Christians began. From 299 to 300, the emperor purged this religious sect out of his palace and later from the army ranks. The Great Persecution of Christians occurred in 303 when he issued the first of three edicts aimed against them. He planned to persecute Christians throughout the whole empire, ordering his co-rulers to eradicate the followers of Jesus from their territories as well. But not all of them thought of Christians as a threat. In the west, only minimal actions were performed against the Christians. In the north, where the community of Christians was small, Constantius wasn't keen on pursuing them. But in Africa, Egypt, Palestine, and other provinces of the east, Christians were severely targeted.

Diocletian retired in 305, and soon, the Tetrarchy collapsed. Of the four rulers, only one was able to keep power and convince the army to follow him. That was the son of Constantius, Flavius Valerius Constantinus. He gained military experience by serving directly under Diocletian and Galerius in their military campaigns in the east. His father died in 306, but not before he called his son to join him in Britannia. There, he was proclaimed the emperor by his father's military forces.

Constantine the Great

Bust of Constantine the Great

When Constantine took over his father's role in Britain, he wasn't recognized as emperor in the rest of the Roman Empire. He had to fight for his right to rule, as the Senate chose Maxentius as the new Augustus of the West. Maxentius was successful in beating Valerius Severus (who had previously been promoted to be Constantine's Caesar) and Galerius. Now, Constantine was able to concentrate on Maxentius, and he challenged the Senate-chosen emperor by calling him a tyrant. Constantine's victory came in 312 when he defeated Maxentius in northern Italy. But the decisive battle occurred later that year, just outside of Rome's walls. Maxentius drowned in the Tiber River while trying to escape the city, and Constantine was now the sole emperor of Rome. His first measure was to forever disband the Praetorian Guard, as they had offered their support to Maxentius.

The sources from which we can learn about Constantine the Great and his rule are tainted by propaganda. As he was seen as the first Christian ruler of Rome, Christian historians painted their writings with allegories that were supposed to convince future generations that Constantine acted by the will of God. Allegedly, his victory over Maxentius convinced Constantine of the truth of Christianity. Before the final battle, he saw the cross symbol across the sun and heard the words "Conquer in this sign." It is believed that since that moment, Constantine decided to paint crosses on the shields of his soldiers, and it was this act that brought him many victories.

But even at this time, Constantine wasn't the only claimant to the throne of Rome. Eastern Europe and Illyricum were held by Valerius Licinianus Licinius, Galerius's successor. The East was held by Maximinus Daia, who was Galerius's nephew. Constantine realized he couldn't fight them both at the same time. Instead, he opted for making an alliance with Licinius against Maximinus. Their attack came as a response to Christian persecution, which Maximinus undertook in 311 and 312. By the end of 313, Constantine and Licinius had defeated Maximinus, and they jointly ruled until 324. However, their rule was not peaceful. They quarreled often, and they even fought briefly in 316/317. The distrust between the two rulers was seen in the fact that they both named their sons Caesar, making it clear they had separate dynastic plans. When Licinius resumed the persecution of Christians in 320, the two rulers became even more estranged.

War was declared in 323 when Constantine moved his troops into the territory under Licinius's rule to counter the invasion of the Goths. It took only one year for Constantine to defeat his rival and take the sole rule of the whole empire. Constantine ruled for another thirteen years, this time as a sole ruler. Instead of Diocletian's Nicomedia, he chose Byzantium as his capital city in the East. He enlarged it and renamed it Constantinople (today's

Istanbul, Turkey). The imperial family and the empire's bureaucracy officially transferred there in 330 CE. Constantinople became the "new Rome." It was positioned on seven hills, and it had fourteen districts. The grain was distributed to the citizens for free, and a huge circus was built so the people could enjoy various games. But aside from its Roman resemblance, Constantinople also had Christian churches that were artistically and architecturally far from Rome's aristocratic ideals. Rome continued to be the cultural center of the empire, where the elite citizens could enjoy their traditions and symbolism, but Rome no longer had its standing army or any political power.

Constantine turned to Christianity, claiming that all of his victories were due to the help of God. However, he didn't officially convert or get baptized until his last days. He claimed he postponed the conversion until he was able to go to the River Jordan, where Jesus himself had been baptized by John the Baptist. However, modern critics believe he wanted the freedom to rule as he saw fit. By being baptized at the end of his life, he could do as he wanted when it came to his rule, as all of his sins would be forgiven. The truth is we will never know for certain why Constantine postponed his conversion, but he is considered the first Christian ruler of the Roman Empire.

The Divide and the Sack of Rome

The generations of emperors after Constantine the Great are known for their power struggles, where brother fought against brother and where many courtiers tried to take the throne as usurpers. Some were more successful than others. During this time, the frontiers of the Roman Empire continued to change. The unrest around the empire's borders prompted the need for shared rule again. Because of the various uprisings and military needs, the emperor was often chosen from the high military ranks. They would then choose their relatives to share the empire with. One would take the West, where the military needs were less, while the other (the one who was considered more capable) would take the East, where he could lead the army to fight against the Sassanids and the Neo-Persian Empire, which, at this point, had risen to its first golden era.

In January 379, Theodosius I (r. 379–395) was elevated to the position of the emperor in the East, even though he had no family ties with the previous ruling dynasty. However, he was chosen by the emperor of the West, Gratian (r. 367–375 with his father and 375–383 as emperor of the West). Theodosius was the son of Gratian's most prominent general, and he was already known for his many military achievements. In the first three years of his rule, he spent time in Thrace, where he fought the invading Gothic tribes. The joint rule of Gratian and Theodosius saw the proclamation of the Nicene Orthodox Christianity (from which major Christian churches, such as Catholic, Orthodox, Lutheran, Anglican, etc., would rise) as the official religion of the empire. Gratian was the one who took away the privileges pagan worshipers had throughout the Roman Empire, and in the city of Rome, he canceled the Vestal Virgin order.

In 383, Gratian was challenged by another military general, Magnus Maximus, who considered himself just as worthy of the rule as Theodosius. Their forces clashed near today's Paris, and Gratian was abandoned by his troops. The fleeing emperor was soon caught and killed, leaving Maximus to seek recognition by Theodosius. Even though Theodosius didn't want to recognize Magnus Maximus as his co-ruler, he didn't have enough power to openly confront him yet. Instead, he stalled with his answer, and by 386, he pretended he recognized some of Maximus's deeds.

However, when the opportunity showed itself in 388, Theodosius gathered his army and moved to the Balkans. In two separate battles, Maximus's army was defeated, and the unrecognized ruler of the West was killed. Theodosius tasked Valentinian II, the younger brother of Gratian, with recovering imperial supremacy in Gaul and Britain, while he remained in Italy until 391. But Valentinian was only a complication for Theodosius's future dynastic plans, as he wanted his own two sons to inherit the empire. In 391, Theodosius received the news of Valentinian's death in southern Gaul. With it, Theodosius became the ruler of both the West and East. But he did not outlive Valentinian for long. He succumbed to an illness in 395, even though he was only in his forties. Nevertheless, he managed to arrange the succession of his two sons, Arcadius, who was to rule the East, and Honorius, who inherited the West. This was the last divide of the Roman Empire, as it would never be reunited again.

Both Arcadius (r. 395–408) and Honorius (r. 395–423) proved to be weak rulers. The brothers were still too young to rule on their own, as Arcadius was a teenager, while his younger brother was only eleven. Later, Arcadius's rule would be marked by his compliance with his wife and counselors, who had all the power. His rule in the East was unremarkable. But in the West, the Visigoths were on the move. As the brothers were still young, and their father had just died, the talented general known as Stilicho the Half-Vandal claimed that Theodosius named him as the regent of both the West and East. He was married to Theodosius's niece Serena for over ten years, and it is possible Theodosius saw him as a capable regent, but there is no evidence to this claim but Stilicho's word. Nevertheless, he found the support he needed in Bishop Ambrose and the poet Claudian, a courtier of Greek origin. But the court in the East would not accept Stilicho as the individual who had authority over both halves of the empire. The internal conflict of the Roman Empire began, and soon, it would produce the rise of Alaricus, better known as Alaric, and the Visigoths.

Alaric was a Goth, and he probably came from the territories of today's Romana and the Danube's Delta. As a youth, he joined the Gothic army, which fought against Rome during the reign of Theodosius I. In 391, he encountered Stilicho for the first time, as this Roman general defended the empire's possessions against the army in which Alaric served. The very next year, the Goths and Rome started living in relative peace, and Alaric took this opportunity to join the Roman army. At this point, Goths were even able to rise in rank and reach elite levels of society through their military distinctions. However, Alaric wasn't satisfied with how Roman generals treated him, and he believed he wasn't given enough recognition for his military successes. He was especially antagonized by the treatment of the Goths during the Battle of the Frigidus (Battle of the Frigid River), in which Theodosius fought the usurper Eugenius in 394. There, many Goths fought and died on both sides, and the Romans celebrated their deaths. Even though Alaric was about to be promoted to the commander of a regular army unit, he declined this reward, doubting Theodosius was an emperor who would treat his kinsmen fairly. Instead, he turned against Constantinople.

In 395, just when Theodosius died, Alaric became the king of the Visigoths. Unfortunately, there are no sources that shed light on exactly how Alaric rose to prominence. Some scholars claim he was a member of the Germanic royal line, while others claim he earned his rank through military endeavors. Nonetheless, his first action was to move his army to Thrace and Macedonia, where they wreaked havoc. There, he was interrupted by Stilicho, who pushed him back toward Epirus.

In Constantinople, Eutropius, a court official who rose to power as Emperor Arcadius's close advisor, condemned Stilicho's efforts against the Visigoths. He thought Stilicho shouldn't have acted without the approval of Arcadius. Eutropius had him proclaimed an enemy of the state. In turn, Stilicho had the Roman Senate do the same to Eutropius. The conflict between the West and East deepened, and Eutropius decided in 397 to proclaim Alaric, a Goth, as the *magister utriusque militiae* (high-ranking officer equivalent to a *strategos*, an army leader, with only the emperor above him as the ultimate military commander) of the Eastern Empire. This position gave Alaric access to Roman military supplies. With the new title and provisions for his troops, Alaric decided to remain quiet for the next few years. In the meantime, the Eastern Empire was successful in fighting off the Huns in Asia Minor.

There is no evidence to explain why Alaric wanted Italy or when he first began his attack, but in 402, he clashed with Stilicho for the second time. Alaric lost at the battle, which was fought near Pollentia (today's Pollenzo), and his whole family was imprisoned. Later, they fought again at Verona, but Stilicho managed to win for the second time. The Roman commander, even though he was victorious, didn't have enough power to destroy Alaric. He was forced to return Alaric's family and to allow the Visigoths to retreat to Pannonia. The Visigoths remained quiet for some time, allowing Stilicho to engage in the internal politics of the empire.

Between 405 and 407, the Western Roman Empire was torn apart by various enemies. In 405, the Goths and other barbarians under King Radagaisus entered northern Italy and started pillaging. A year later, the invasion of the Vandals and the Silingi occurred when they crossed the Rhine (coming from Silesia in today's Poland). Alaric saw the opportunity to invade, as Stilicho was in no position to fight three enemies at the same time. He marched to the north of the empire and stationed his army in Noricum (today's Austria). There, he threatened an invasion of Italy unless he was paid 4,000 pounds of gold and granted permission to settle his army in Pannonia. Stilicho agreed. To complicate things further, the emperor of the Eastern Empire, Arcadius, died in 408, leaving behind his seven-year-old son as his successor. Stilicho wanted to take the opportunity in the East to install his son as a ruler there. For this, he was executed by Emperor Honorius.

With Stilicho's death, Alaric was left without his 4,000 pounds of gold. So, he once more raised an army and marched to Italy. This time, he didn't satisfy himself by pillaging the northern towns. Instead, he turned his forces toward Rome. By 408, Alaric had Rome surrounded. Because the king of the Visigoths had control of the Tiber River, the city was starving. And with the hunger came disorder. Christians blamed pagans and vice versa, and the poor blamed the elite. The Senate found a scapegoat in Stilicho's wife, accusing her of conspiring with Alaric. Emperor Honorius was at Ravenna at the time, and the Senate was left alone to make a decision. They opted for negotiations. But Alaric's price was too high, as he demanded all the gold and all the silver of the city, as well as the freedom for all barbarian slaves. Honorius declined these terms once he received a delegation from Rome. Instead, he moved the troops from Dalmatia to come and relieve Rome. Unfortunately, they were ambushed by Alaric, and all but one hundred died.

The negotiations continued and dragged on for two more years until another leader of the Goths decided to intervene. This man was Sarus of the Amali dynasty, and he served under Stilicho during his efforts against Alaric. It is not known why he meddled in the affairs, but Sarus's appearance angered Alaric, who decided to sack Rome. On August 24th, 410, the Goths entered the city. According to Christian tradition, the Goths were believers at this point, and since Rome was protected by God, they did His bidding and decided not to capture it. Instead, they opted for "gentle and caring" plunder, taking care not to hurt anyone. The Christian legend about the sacking of Rome speaks of Goths who peacefully took what they considered their reward, while it was God who sent thunderbolts to destroy the pagan constructions, such as the mausoleums of Augustus and Hadrian and the old imperial palaces. Alaric ordered that the citizens who were sheltering in the church should be spared. The Goths were painted as merciful Christians who only brought about the wrath of God upon Rome. Even though there are no accounts to claim otherwise, the historical event of the sacking of

Rome was most likely completely different from the Christian stories and legends.

Alaric certainly traumatized the Roman world by attacking its "Eternal City." However, he gained nothing politically by sacking Rome. He spent only three days within the city walls when famine struck, as the grain supply from Africa had been halted. He decided to lead his forces there and get the grain himself. But while he was sailing to Sicily, he became very ill. The Gothic commanders decided to take him north, and in early 411, Alaric died at Consentia in Bruttium (today's Calabria, Italy).

Chapter 7 – The Fall of the West; The East Thrives

Rome didn't fall in a day, nor was it due to an invasion or occupation. Rome's fall was a long process. Scholars often place the fall of Rome in 476, as that was the year when the last Roman emperor ended his rule in the West. There is no single reason for this downfall even though many historians and scientists have tried to answer it. Environmental problems, disease, dysgenic breeding, wars, lead poisoning from the pipes, economic stagnation, and many more reasons have been put forward. However, the most probable answer is that Rome fell due to a series of unfortunate events and the government's inability to react to them.

After the death of Alaric, his brother-in-law, Athaulf, took over the leadership of the Visigoths. But even though he tried, he could not make Honorius capitulate. In 412, he changed his political views and left Italy, leading his people to Gaul. This was the time of internal struggles when the Western Empire began to crumble. The barbaric tribes of the Alans, Vandals, and Suebi invaded Gaul, prompting Athaulf to search for an alliance with Honorius. In Britannia, a military commander named Flavius Claudius Constantinus proclaimed himself an emperor in 407. He raised an army and launched an attack on Gaul, where he defeated Honorius's troops so badly that the Western emperor had to admit his authority. In 409, he even proclaimed Constantinus a co-emperor. After that year, he was known as Constantine III. However, the two emperors did not rule in peace. They were constantly fighting and trying to assert dominion over each other. In 411, Honorius sent his troops to clash with Constantine III in Spain. Constantine III was defeated and executed. In 410, in Britannia, a rebellion against Constantine's officials who had remained there occurred. When the Brits asked for the help of Emperor Honorius, they were told that they should look after themselves from now and raise their defenses. This was a clear sign that Honorius had given up on Britannia as a Roman province, and in British history, 410 is the year when Britain claimed its independence.

When Honorius died in 423, the only heir to the Western Empire was Constantine III's son, Valentinian III. Since he was still a child, his mother, Galla Placidia, became the regent. She was the daughter of Theodosius I, and even though her son started his sole rule in 437, she remained a major figure in Rome's politics until she died in 450. During her regency, the Western Roman Empire deteriorated exponentially. The first territories to be lost were in the Diocese of Africa (all the North African provinces of Rome), which was soon followed by Gaul. Hispania started slipping out of the empire's grip with the rise of the local rulers, while in the northeast, the Franks started stirring.

By 434, in the court at Ravenna where Valentinian III ruled, Galla Placidia started relying on her new *magister militum*, Flavius Aetius. He was so efficient as a military commander that he quickly gained the loyalty of his troops. He was also an avid politician, and it is no wonder he managed to assert his control over the whole of Italy. He rose through the ranks quickly while pacifying the Goths and regaining territories such as the West Balkans, Africa

Proconsularis, Byzacena, Gallia Narbonensis Viennensis, and the territories of today's Loire Valley in France. But he never managed to retrieve northern Gaul, as the border at the Rhine collapsed. Spain was in the same situation as northern Gaul. There, a large kingdom of Suebi arose, and they allied themselves with the Visigoths settled around Garonne (northern Spain). Flavius Aetius planned on retrieving all the lost territories, but the remaining Roman army wasn't enough. He needed to recruit barbarians from outside of the Roman borders.

Flavius Aetius managed to return some of the territories in Gaul by 436, and then he concentrated his forces on Spain, where he campaigned until 448. But Spain proved to be a much tougher task. Even though the Roman campaigns went very well at the beginning, the Suebi leader Rechiar allied himself with the bagaudae (a band of organized peasant insurgents) and the Visigoths by marrying one of Alaric's great-granddaughters. There was nothing more Flavius could do, as he had no force to fight the allied barbarians.

In 450, the West had something else to worry about. Attila the Hun had just given up on conquering Constantinople and was about to invade the Western Roman Empire. However, the older sister of Emperor Valentinian III, Honoria, secretly wrote a letter to Attila, offering herself in marriage. She was unsatisfied with her brother's choice, as he planned on marrying her to a low-born politician. Attia accepted her proposal and demanded Valentinian to give him his sister and half of the Western Empire as her dowry. When the court at Ravenna declined his demand, Attila had an excuse to start a war, claiming he was only defending the honor of his future bride. Galla Placidia meddled, as she would not give her daughter to a barbarian. Instead, she forcefully married her daughter to a Roman politician, Bassus Herculanus. The same year, the influential Galla Placidia died.

Attila the Hun

The territories controlled by the Huns under Attila
*Slovenski Volk, CC BY-SA 3.0 <https://creativecommons.org/licenses/by-sa/3.0>, via
Wikimedia Commons https://commons.wikimedia.org/wiki/File:Huns450.png*

After gaining an excuse to attack the Western Roman Empire, Attila the Hun gathered his forces and crossed the Rhine. He destroyed several cities before he arrived at the Loire. There, he was met by the grand force gathered by Flavius Aetius, who had made several alliances with the Goths, Franks, Alans, and some of the Gallic bagaudae, who had crossed to the Roman side and started calling themselves Aremoricani. This multiethnic army of Flavius Aetius was enough to halt the progress of the Huns. On June 21st, 451, the forces finally clashed at the Battle of the Catalaunian Fields, a place that modern scholars speculate could have been between Troyes and Châlons-Sur-Marne (modern-day Châlons-en-Champagne). There were many casualties. The contemporary bishop and chronicler of the events, Hydatius, states there were as many as 300,000 dead. The *Gallic Chronicle of 511* agrees with him, but instead of the precise number, it gives the description of innumerable cadavers covering the battlefield. While Theodoric I, the leader of the Gauls, was killed in the battle, Attila's forces lost more than the Romans. The Huns were forced to retreat to Pannonia. There were many attempts to reconstruct the battle, but the lack of sources makes it hard to conclude who was victorious. Even though Attila was forced to retreat, it is possible he inflicted enough damage to the Roman army to call a victory. However, most of the scholars agree the victory belonged to the Romans or, at the very least, the outcome of the battle was indecisive. Whatever the case was, the Romans didn't chase the Huns, and the very next year, Attila renewed his attacks on Italy.

Although Attila took Aquileia, Mediolanum, and Ticinum, he never pressed into Rome. The Christian legend says that Pope Leo I talked the Huns out of sacking Rome, while modern historians speculate that Attila was paid not to attack the Eternal City. Another possibility was that Attila's army was decimated by malaria and dysentery, which were common in Italy at that time. In 453, the Huns returned to their heartland across the Danube. The same year, Attila died under strange circumstances. He died while celebrating his new marriage and drinking heavily. While some accounts say how the great Hun leader choked while having a nosebleed, others claim he was poisoned. Later, the legends of his death started merging with the truth, making it impossible to know what happened.

The death of Attila the Hun meant the end for the Huns. Soon, they were attacked by the Germanic tribes, and to protect themselves, they asked to step into the service of the Roman Empire. With the Huns now in Pannonia, the rise of the Ostrogoths occurred, and soon they settled all over the Balkans. Attila had been the greatest threat to Rome since Hannibal in the 3rd century BCE, but the Eternal City was lucky this time. Flavius Aetius met his end by Emperor Valentinian III's hand after he became involved in some political intrigue in 454. However, the emperor did not live long either. In 455, he was assassinated by two bodyguards of the deceased Aetius. There is no evidence to support the theory that they were avenging their master. It is more likely they had another motive. Petronius Maximus had risen to power, and he even married Valentinian's widow, Licinia Eudoxia. It is possible that he bribed the two bodyguards to assassinate the emperor.

The End of the Western Roman Empire

The Anglo-Saxon scholar the Venerable Bede (c. 673–735) wrote that the Western Roman Empire ended with the death of Emperor Valentinian III. However, this is not how modern scholars interpret events. The period of dismay and havoc certainly started at this point. Some individuals fought to preserve what was left of the Western Roman Empire, but the arrival of the Vandal fleet near Ostia in May of 455 deterred their plans. Rome was sacked for the second time, and Petronius Maximus was killed after his brief rule. Their leader, Gaiseric, took Eudocia, the daughter of Valentinian III, so she could be married to his son Huneric. This proved to be crucial for the survival of Rome; if they had a son, he would be a legitimate successor to the throne. But at the moment, no one ruled Rome. Avitus, an ambassador of Petronius Maximus, was proclaimed emperor while he was serving at the court of Gothic King Theodoric II. However, he didn't last for long. In a rebellion instigated by his military commanders Majorian and Ricimer, Avitus was defeated and captured, but he was not killed. Instead, he was forced to become a bishop and denounce the throne. The empire now belonged to Majorian.

Rome put her hopes in Majorian, as he seemed to be a good emperor. At the beginning of his rule, he easily defeated the Alemanni and Vandals, and he quelled a rebellion among the Goths. In 458, he even managed to reintegrate the Gauls in the Roman Empire through diplomatic means. In May 460, Majorian focused on Spain, where the situation with the Vandals was intensifying. Unfortunately, Gaiseric's Vandals were impossible to defeat, and the emperor had to sue for peace. He was forced to accept a shameful settlement by which he would recognize that Mauritania belonged to the Vandals. As soon as he set foot on Italian ground, his "friend" Ricimer apprehended him and executed him for treason on August 2nd, 461.

But Ricimer didn't want the throne for himself—at least not openly. He took the time to choose a person who he could manipulate, as he wanted to rule from the shadows. Finally, he installed Senator Libius Severus (Severus III), but hardly anyone accepted the legitimacy of his rule. King Aegidius of the Franks, Warlord Marcellinus of Dalmatia, and King Gaiseric of the Visigoths all refused to recognize Severus as the emperor. Nevertheless, Libius managed to rule for the next four years, though it was unremarkable. When he died in 465 (circumstances unknown), the Western Roman Empire had no ruler for the next two years. Since the court in Ravenna couldn't agree on who should rule them, they asked Eastern Emperor Leo I to intervene. Leo installed Procopius Anthemius (r. 467–472), a high-born court official of the Eastern Roman Empire.

During his reign, Anthemius tried to solve the problem of the Vandals. He dedicated 64,000 pounds of gold and 700,000 pounds of silver to this effort. With such expenses, he assembled a mighty armada composed of 1,100 ships, which were used to transport the Roman army to Africa. The main commander of the armada was the brother-in-law of Emperor Leo I, Flavius Basiliscus (the future emperor of the Eastern Roman Empire). But the Romans didn't plan on only attacking by sea. They also gathered a large land force, which was to enter the Vandal territory through Libya. The third point of attack was to be at Sardinia, where a smaller fleet would be deployed.

The initial attacks on the Vandals were successful. Sardinia and Sicily were captured, the enemy was expelled from Tripolitania, and Gaiseric's naval force was defeated. However, Basiliscus allowed the Vandals to have five days of a ceasefire, which Gaiseric exploited to bring in the main force of his fleet. Basiliscus's navy was decimated, and the Vandals took back both Sardinia and Sicily. The expensive campaign against the Vandals was a disaster, but it didn't remove Procopius Anthemius from the Western throne. Ricimer tried to dispose of him, but he was unable to do much since Anthemius controlled the standing army.

Meanwhile, in Gaul, things were changing. King Theodoric II was killed by his brother, Euric. The new king of the Goths had no love for Rome, and he decided to lead his people into an open rebellion. Anthemius had no other choice but to send his son, Anthemiolus, to deal with Euric. Little did he know he sent his son to die. Euric proved capable, and after disposing of Anthemiolus, his troops took Avaricum (modern-day Bourges).

Ricimer was happy to hear of Euric's success, as this meant Procopius Anthemius was weakened. It was a good time to attack. Under the persistent siege, Rome capitulated, and Anthemius was caught and beheaded on July 11th, 472. Even before dealing with Anthemius, Ricimer proclaimed Anicius Olybrius as the new emperor. He was the brother-in-law of Huneric, the son of King Gaiseric of the Vandals, which brought the Vandals hope that they would legitimately take over Rome. However, Olybrius was yet another puppet ruler of Ricimer, and he didn't last for more than a few months. He died of lung edema, disappointing the Vandals. Ricimer died only a month after Anthemius, coughing blood due to a hemorrhage.

With Ricimer's death, there was no one capable of holding power in Rome. Several emperors appeared and disappeared rather quickly, leaving Rome in tatters. Ironically, the last Western Roman emperor was named Romulus, just like the founder of the Eternal City. He ruled as Romulus Augustulus (475–476), but his empire consisted of only Italy and southern provinces. The rest was lost to the Goths, Visigoths, and Vandals during the rules of Romulus's incapable predecessors. Romulus proved unable to administer, as he had no support from the military. In fact, in August 476, the Germanic commander of the Roman troops, Odoacer, raised a mutiny, taking Rome for himself. But he spared Romulus, putting him under house arrest. Later, Romulus would go to the monastery in Campania, where he would remain until the end of his life.

For the first time in history, Rome was ruled by a barbarian emperor. This is the moment that marks the end of the Western Roman Empire. However, the fall wasn't a fall. The empire didn't simply cease to exist. It was more of a transition, and it is highly debatable if the people of Rome even cared who ruled them at this point. To them, whether the emperor was a Roman, Goth, or Vandal meant nothing more than a distant name. Life continued for the common people and even the elite. They proceeded to work the land, buy and sell goods, write poetry, and build glorious architectural wonders. Culturally, Rome never fell. And it is in the culture and art that we see the transformation and transition from the Western Roman Empire to simply Rome. There were no city ruins on which to build a new one. The empire ended, but Rome didn't fall. Through its culture, it expanded to the whole of Europe, where it still survives.

In the East

While Flavius Aetius ruled the Western Roman Empire in all but name, Theodosius II reigned from 408 until 450 in Constantinople. After the death of his father, Arcadius, Theodosius was proclaimed as the emperor, even though he was only seven years old. Priscus of Panium, the 5th-century historian, described the emperor as a weak, cowardly man who would rather buy his empire out of trouble than employ its army. Modern historians find the justification for Theodosius's weakness in his education. Throughout his life, Theodosius was guided by his overly pious sister, Aelia Pulcheria, who ruled the empire as his regent. She was a devoted Christian who used religion and her virginity, rather than marriage, to gain political power. She devoted herself to the cult of the Virgin Mary and gained strong influence among the courtiers. However, if anyone was to go against her, it meant they would go against the Mother of God. She was well protected, and she gained control over her younger brother's education. Theodosius learned religious texts by heart, and he often debated them with bishops and clerks. Together with his sister, Theodosius II turned his court into something resembling a monastery. The royal siblings would rise at dawn to sing the divine hymns before resuming their daily obligations.

Such a pious emperor was easily persuaded by his sister to start a war against the Sassanids, who were persecuting the Christians at the time. Aelia Pulcheria even took it upon herself to find a suitable wife for her brother. She chose a high-born Greek orphan named Athenais. Though she was initially a pagan, the girl agreed to be baptized to marry the emperor. She even took a Christian name, Aelia Eudocia. By 423, the couple had their first child, a daughter named Luciana Eudoxia, who would later marry Valentinian III, the ruler of the Western Roman Empire.

Theodosius II was also the founder of the University of Constantinople in 425, which taught mathematics, geography, law, astronomy, music, and rhetoric. But his reign is probably most known for the theological dispute that occurred when he proclaimed Nestorius, a monk from Syria, as the Bishop of Constantinople. Nestorius's religious views clashed with those of Aelia Pulcheria, as he wanted to divide Christ by his two natures: the holy Christ, the son of God, and the human Christ, the son of the Virgin Mary. He wanted to rename the Virgin Mary to *Christotokos* ("Mother of Christ") from the previous *Theotokos* ("Mother of God"). Finally, Theodosius summoned the Council of Ephesus in 431, which resulted in the deposition of Nestorius as bishop and his banishment in exile. Even though Pulcheria had no official influence over the council, she was celebrated as the strength of Orthodoxy in the East.

Theodosius II died in a riding accident, leaving his sister with the responsibility toward the empire. He had already divorced his wife, and the pair had no male heir. So, it was upon Pulcheria to find a suitable husband who would continue to rule the empire. She settled for a Thracian military officer, Flavius Marcianus (better known as Marcian; r. 450–457). The couple married under the condition that he would not violate Pulcheria so she could remain chaste.

Immediately after the coronation, Marcian had to face the biggest challenge in Constantinople's history: the Hunnic invasion under the leadership of the famous Attila the Hun. The heartland of Attila's power was in Pannonia, north of the Danube (today's Hungary and North Serbia), which the Huns had settled in the early 5th century by destroying Viminacium and Sirmium. The Huns never intended to settle within the borders of the Roman Empire. They saw the opportunity to extort blackmail money from Constantinople by constantly invading the borders of the Eastern Empire. But Marcian wanted to put an end to the extortion Attila demanded. The new emperor wanted to retake the Balkans, but to do that, he needed money. So, he simply stopped paying the Huns. Luckily for him, Attila did not attack Marcian. He instead decided the Western Empire was a much easier target. With this move, Marcian gained time to establish peace and prosperity throughout his realm. Once Attila died in 453, the Eastern Empire was relieved from the Hunnic pressure, and the new prosperity allowed Marcian to cut some taxes.

Marcian's rule left the empire's treasury with a surplus when he died in 457. Since he had no children with Aelia Pulcheria, he wanted his son-in-law, Procopius Anthemius, to be his successor. Later, Anthemius would become the Western emperor, taking Marcian's daughter to be his empress. The court scheming resulted in the installation of Leo I as the emperor in the East. He was of Dacian origin, and he was supposed to be a puppet ruler, as he was installed by the military commander Flavius Ardabur Aspar. However, Leo I gained his independence, killed Aspar, and proved to be a capable emperor during his twenty-year-long reign.

To gain the alliance of Isaurians (they inhabited the mountainous region of southern Asia Minor), Leo I married his daughter Ariadne to their leader Tarasikodissa, later known as Emperor Zeno. This man became Leo's confidant, and he was promptly elevated to the position of *praefectus praetorio* (which was only an administrative office by this point) of the East. In 468, Leo tried to deal with the Vandals and sent an armada against them, but this effort was a complete failure. In 474, he tried to take over the Western part of the empire by sending Julius Nepos, the commander of the Balkan forces, to take over the rule from Glycerius. However, Leo I died in February the same year, and his successor, Leo II, took over in November.

Zeno was installed as the protector of young Leo II. But after his protege died in 474, Zeno assumed control over the Eastern Empire, and he ruled until 491. His reign was marked by numerous domestic revolts, and early in his reign, he had to deal with the usurper Basiliscus, who was proclaimed the emperor at Constantinople. As early as 475, Zeno was exiled due to court intrigue, and Basiliscus started ruling alongside his son, Marcus. However, the co-emperors indulged in Hermeticism, and soon they found themselves in the Church's disfavor. Zeno came back and continued his rule, outliving his counterparts in the West. Zeno ruled in Constantinople when the last king of the Western Roman Empire was overthrown by Odoacer. The fall of the Western Empire brought change to the East too. It effectively became the Byzantine Empire, and a new era was about to start with the reign of Justinian I. It was the beginning of the 6th century and the end of what modern scholars call antiquity.

Chapter 8 – Rome in the Middle Ages

Justinian and the End of Antiquity

At the end of what historians designate as antiquity, the Eastern Roman Empire went through one of its most important and successful phases. Although modern historians refer to the Eastern Roman Empire as the Byzantine Empire, this term was first coined to represent the survival of the East when the West fell. The transformation (rather than fall) of the Western Roman Empire had a strong influence on the East. While the West fell under the influence of foreign, barbarian rulers, the East thrived and prospered. It rose from being just one part of the Roman Empire to the Byzantine Empire.

The most important emperor of this phase was Justinian I (527–565). As a nephew of his predecessor, Emperor Justin I, young Justinian received an outstanding education. He was especially interested in Roman law, history, and theology. By 527, the year he was made co-emperor next to his ailing uncle, Justinian was already successful as a politician, having served the empire as a consul since 521. The most influential person in Justinian's life was his wife, Theodora. She is a point of controversy, as she was a low-born ex-actress who also indulged in prostitution. She was hated by their contemporaries, but Justinian often turned to her for advice. Later, she was described as being a capable and very intelligent empress.

Another person of interest during the reign of Emperor Justinian I was John the Cappadocian. He was a finance minister of Byzantium, and as such, he came up with a new taxation program, which was so efficient that it solely funded the war with the Sassanian Empire. Although he implemented taxes that extracted money from both the rich and poor, John did enormous work on weeding out the corruption from the empire's infrastructure. However, John the Cappadocian was extremely unpopular in his own time, while today's scholars see his economic methods as innovative and brave.

Justinian was an avid supporter of the Nicene Orthodoxy. During his reign, other religions were often persecuted, as he legalized the suppression of all non-Christian religions. But his greatest achievement was the reformation and standardization of the Roman law. Before Justinian, Roman law was an unorganized bunch of legislatures, which were opened to interpretation. What he did was gather and unify all the laws, eradicate the confusing parts, and replace them with a concise and effective legal system supported by a series of statutes. However, his view of the law strongly reflected the Christian values of the 6th century. It was completed in 529 CE, and the *Corpus Juris Civilis* ("Body of Civil Law") still influences the modern law of many European countries.

Although Justinian was a successful reformer, his rule didn't escape internal struggles. In 532, in Constantinople, riots broke out in the streets. They are known as the Nika Riots, in which two rival factions of chariot racers, the Blues and the Greens, united against the emperor. Justinian had the habit of employing very unpopular but efficient advisors. Besides John the Cappadocian, there was Tribonian, who was the supervisor of the law reforms. While John was hated for his implementation of the taxes onto the poor,

Tribonian was unpopular because of his corruption. In Constantinople, the chariot races were very popular, and the games took part in a hippodrome, which could house a great number of people. The supporters of either the Blue or Green team would break between games to shout their political demands to the emperor, who would also be present and enjoying the races (Justinian supported the Blues). During one such game, the supporters of the two teams united and rioted, demanding the dismissal of John and Tribonian as imperial advisors. The riots turned violent, and several people lost their lives. Seven ringleaders were sentenced to death and executed on January 12th, 532. The following day, when Justinian declared the opening of the games (as was the custom), he faced an angry and volatile crowd who demanded his abdication. Justinian contemplated leaving the city for his safety, but he was persuaded by his wife to stay. He then ordered the complete and brutal suppression of the riots.

Under the pressure of the rioters, Justinian did dismiss John the Cappadocian and Tribonian, but the riots continued. He ordered Generals Belisarius and Mundus to crush the insurrections, and more than 30,000 people died in the attempt. The generals were brutal, and they trapped both team factions in a hippodrome and started the slaughter. The riots were over, but the emperor had to deal with those senators who supported them. The most important among them was Hypatius, who was chosen by the crowd to replace Justinian on the Byzantine throne. He was executed, while other senators were exiled. The riots later got their name because the angry crowd was chanting "Nika," the Greek word for victory.

The Reconquest of Africa and Italy

When the Western Roman Empire fell to the barbarians, their leader, Odoacer, swore allegiance to Zeno, who ruled in Constantinople at the time. But Odoacer and the later Ostrogoth successors continued to rule Italy independently. Rome was administered by the senators, who, in reality, lost their legislative and executive powers. The pope continued to be elected in Rome as the Christian leader of the empire, and he was usually a descendant of the senatorial families. The situation in Italy continued to develop independently from the Byzantine Empire until 353 when Ostrogoth King Theodahad arrested and killed his cousin, Queen Amalaswintha, who had acted as the regent of the Ostrogoths. The cousins had ruled Italy as equals up until this point, but Theodahad was now proclaimed a usurper.

This political instability within Italy gave the Byzantine Empire an excuse to attack and return what was left of the Western Roman Empire to their fold. However, before turning his attention to Italy, Justinian chose to deal with North Africa, where he sent General Belisarius to recapture the territories now ruled by the Vandals. In 533, Justinian organized a triumph for Belisarius, as he had managed to wrestle the African provinces out of the enemy's hands. Many of the Vandals captured during this conflict joined the Byzantine army, and with their help, Justinian managed to recapture the city of Rome in 536.

But Rome wasn't the capital of the Ostrogoth rulers of Italy. The court continued to be in Ravenna, and it would take another four years for the Byzantines to capture it. The Ostrogoths didn't want to give up Rome so easily, so they laid down a siege that lasted for over a year (537–538). But Belisarius proved his ability to command not just the army but also the whole city. He persevered in Rome and crushed the siege. By 340, he had taken Ravenna too. Italy was once more in the hands of its Roman descendants, though it was now ruled from faraway Constantinople. However, the fighting was far from over. The Ostrogoths rebelled and captured Rome in 546 (the third sack of Rome), but Belisarius managed to retrieve it quickly. Rome was again attacked and taken by its Gothic masters in 549. In 552, another Byzantine military commander, Narses, reconquered it for the last time.

Rome struggled during the Gothic Wars of the 530s and 540s, which ravaged much of Italy. Rome itself was demolished to the point where no aqueducts were in working order. Disease broke out among the citizens, and the population was decimated. Legend has it that, at one point, Rome was completely abandoned, and no one except the rats lived in it. However, this legend is highly unlikely. Justinian organized famine relief efforts and also sent workers from the Byzantine Empire to repair Rome's water supply. He even reorganized the Senate, giving them back much of the executive power, but they were obliged to report to Constantinople and its representatives in Ravenna. Some scholars argue that Justinian saved Rome, but the question remains if it needed saving. If Byzantium hadn't meddled, there is no way of saying if Italy would have been destroyed by the internal struggles of its Ostrogoth rulers or if it would have thrived by taking some other political and/or cultural courses.

The Justinian Plague

In 541, the Byzantine Empire was hit by a new and strange disease. It probably came through Egypt, but how it exactly started remains unknown. The disease quickly spread across the Mediterranean region, and it took the lives of all levels of society. No one was spared. Poor or rich, people suffered from fever, weakness, and painful skin lesions caused by swelling lymph nodes. Contemporary medics and historians took care to precisely describe the symptoms, and based on these accounts, modern scholars believe that the first-ever pandemic of the bubonic plague erupted. This disease is caused by a bacterium, *Yersinia pestis*, which was probably brought to Constantinople by rats who lived on the ships that supplied the capital with Egyptian grain.

The first pandemic lasted for 200 years, as people of that period didn't have developed medicine or hygienic habits to fight it. Historian Procopius notes that in Constantinople alone, 10,000 people died each day during the first year of the plague. Whether this is an exaggeration or not remains unknown, but Constantinople soon lacked healthy people who would be able to produce and distribute food. This, in turn, led to a secondary crisis, the famine. The city struggled and had no idea how to stop the menace. In turn, the plague spread through other parts of Europe, and by the end of its 200-year ravage, it took more than half of the total population of the continent.

In 542, Emperor Justinian himself got sick. Contemporary sources claim he contracted the deadly bubonic plague and that he survived. However, modern scholars can't confirm this claim, though it is highly likely. He continued his rule from Constantinople until 565 when he died, leaving the Byzantine Empire in the hands of his nephew Justin. The plague continued, and it would often reappear until the mid-8th century. In the 14th century, it would come to Europe's shores again with a similar, perhaps even worse, outcome. This is known as the Black Death.

The Formation of the Papal States

The early medieval history of Italy is dominated by the Lombards, a Germanic people who appeared in the Italian Peninsula from Pannonia around 568. The Lombards never conquered the whole peninsula, and Italy would be in disunity for the next fourteen centuries. After 600 CE, the Lombards occupied around two-thirds of the peninsula, while the rest was in the possession of the Byzantine Empire, mostly centered around Ravenna, Rome, Naples, and the southern territories of the Italian mainland. Under the Lombard pressure, the Byzantine Empire was forced to reorganize its Italian possessions into an exarchate. This means that each duchy (Rome, Naples, Venetia, Calabria, Perugia, etc.) was a part of a larger political entity headed by a Byzantine official known as an exarch.

It remains unknown how the first exarchs acted. The presumption is that this position was at first strictly military. But in time, exarchs started assuming some of the civil functions. They were always sent from Constantinople; no exarch was ever born in Italy. The exarch was the emperor's direct representative in Ravenna, and as such, he was always appointed from among the high-ranking officers of the palace administration. During the 6th century, the exarchates were very unstable. The threat of collapse was always present, as these exarchates sued for independence. However, it remained unified for quite some time due to the shared religious and civic institutions.

Within the Byzantine possessions in Italy, the Roman Church had a special place. It was much older than the duchies and exarchates, and as such, it held tremendous power. During the early Lombard invasion, the Church took upon itself to care for the orphans and widows left behind by the defenders of the Byzantine Empire. Soon, the Church needed access to the water supply and public health to care for the people. This allowed the Church to further become in charge of the public spectacles and urban conveniences. The Roman Church had to organize a system of ecclesiastical courts to divide its ever-growing responsibility. Soon enough, the Church started ruling in civil cases and made peace between the local magnates. By the early 7th century, Byzantine Italy found itself relying on the Roman Church's government. During that same time, the Church became the largest landholder in Italy. The papal government and these land possessions equaled power. It is no wonder the Church was the instigator of the religious separation between the West and the East.

The first emperor to forbid the use of religious images (icons) was Leo III (717–741). His reasons for putting an end to the practice of iconoclasm (the veneration of icons) are unknown, but many speculate that he was influenced by Islam. However, it is more likely he wanted to appease the non-Christians within his empire who had become agitated by his forceful Christianization of the Jews in 722. Leo gained the support of the upper classes of society but was strongly opposed by the monks and various religious leaders. Even the patriarch of Constantinople, Germanus I, resigned after Leo III issued the edict against iconoclasm. In the West, Pope Gregory II strongly opposed the emperor's decision and even went so far as to completely ignore the new law.

The pope had no reason to fear Leo's retaliation, as the armies of Ravenna, Venice, and Pentapolis rose up in 727 and declared they would defend him against the iconoclastic policy. This was the first divide between the Church and the city officials still loyal to the emperor in Constantinople. Iconoclasm was a cause that united the people of the Italian exarchate, who openly declared the end of Byzantine rule. Finally, the traditional desires for the autonomy of the Italian provinces became evident. But this was just the beginning. A long struggle between the papal and imperial factions in Ravenna would occur before the destiny of the Italian Peninsula was decided.

During this time, Rome and its Church fought the renewed attacks of the Lombards. To punish the pope for his disobedience of the iconoclasm edict, Leo III allied himself with the Lombards. Having no other options, Pope Gregory III asked the Franks for help. He sent a missive to Frankish King Charles Martel (r. 718–741), asking for his help to defend the St. Peter's Basilica. Even though he was only a religious leader, the pope wrote to Charles as if he was an equal, as a head of the state. Between 739 and 742, there is no evidence of Lombard attacks, and it is unknown how Charles responded to the pope's letter. However, many years later, Charlemagne did mention that his grandfather, Charles Martel, defended the Holy Roman Church.

The iconoclasm issue continued during the reign of Leo's successor, Constantine V. Although he succeeded his father after he died in 741, Constantine V lost the throne the next year when his brother-in-law, Artabasdos, challenged him. Artabasdos again legalized the worship of the icons, but Constantine V was back on the throne in 743. He immediately returned his father's policy of iconoclasm, instigating hostilities between Rome and Constantinople.

After the Lombards took Ravenna in 751, Pope Stephen II was forced to ask Frankish King Pepin the Short (r. 751–768) for help. He traveled to Francia, where he crowned Pepin as king and *patricius Romanorum*, the protector of Rome, in 754. Together, they came back to Italy. Pepin was successful in recapturing the papal possessions, which included the city of Rome. Pepin's capture and donation of the Italian cities to the pope allowed the Papal States to rise. The Papal States were Italian territories under the direct rule of the Holy Roman Church from 754 until 1870.

When Pope Leo III decided to crown Charlemagne, the son and successor of Pepin the Short, as the "Emperor of the Romans" in 800, the people of Constantinople rebelled. They considered their emperors to be the direct successors of the Roman Empire. To make peace, Charlemagne offered to marry Queen Irene of Byzantium, but before she could accept, she was deposed from her position of regent to her son, Constantine V.

The Byzantine Empire and the Great Schism

The Byzantine Empire, 8th century

With the coronation of Charlemagne as the "Emperor of the Romans," Pope Leo III started the much greater political separation of the West and East. The West eventually became the Holy Roman Empire, but the Byzantine Empire continued to thrive in the East. There, the ancient spirit of Rome continued with a series of quick successions of often unrelated emperors. During the mid-8th century, the Byzantine Empire had to deal with the Bulgar threat coming. The Bulgars were a Turkic people who settled in the vicinity of the Byzantine Empire, taking over territories like today's Bulgaria. For the next several centuries, the Bulgars would have a direct influence on Byzantine's destiny.

When the Bulgarian Empire started expanding its borders and taking the territories of Serbia and Macedonia, the Byzantines renewed the conflict. As the Bulgarian Empire grew, so did its threat to the Byzantines. It was Emperor Michael III (r. 842-867) who successfully put a stop to iconoclasm and who spread Christianity to the Slavic nations in Great Moravia. The Bulgarian Empire was under the direct influence of the Franks, and Michael didn't want to lose the opportunity to convert them to Christianity too. In 864, he invaded Bulgaria to impose the Eastern rites on their leader, Boris I. Boris was successfully baptized the next year in Constantinople.

Michael III gained the reputation of a brave military leader, but in the centuries to come, his image would constantly be related to personal dissipation. His successors and political opponents called him "Michael the Sot" or "Michael the Drunken," but beyond their propaganda material, there is no evidence to confirm this emperor's wild nature and his pursuits for pleasure. In 866, Michael decided to raise his personal friend, known as Basil the Macedonian, to the position of co-emperor. Basil's nickname, "the Macedonian," is misleading, as his origins were in Armenia. But during the Bulgarian raids, his family was relocated north of the Danube, where many

Macedonians took refuge. Thus, Basil's family was confused for one of the Macedonian families.

Basil claimed that Michael's debauchery led him to turn against his friend and plot his assassination. When Basil became the sole ruler of the Byzantine Empire in 867, he started the so-called Macedonian dynasty. Their imperial line would rule until 1056. During their rule, the Byzantine Empire retrieved much of its previous territories that had been lost in the Arab conquests of the 7th century. It was also the period of the beginning of Macedonian art and letters, when the Byzantine Empire showed increased interest in its ancient Hellenistic past. They would masterfully connect classical art to contemporary Christian values.

Probably the most distinguished ruler of the Macedonian dynasty was Basil II (r. 976-1025). He was the son of Emperor Romanos II (r. 945-963), but since he was still a child when his father died, the Byzantine Empire was in the hands of two powerful regents. The first, Nikephoros II Phokas, was a military general who married Basil's mother after the death of Romanos II. However, Nikephoros died in 969 and was succeeded by Emperor John I Tzimiskes, who ruled as a senior to young Emperor Basil II. Tzimiskes suddenly died in 976. Since Basil had just turned eighteen, he was able to assume the role of senior emperor. Since he was still very young and inexperienced, he was influenced by his uncle, a eunuch named Basil Lekapenos.

While Basil II let his uncle run the empire for the first nine years of his rule, he took the opportunity to gain experience in administration and the military. When he felt he was ready, Basil got rid of his uncle by exiling him. Finally, he started his sole rule in 985, with his younger brother Constantine VIII as co-ruler but only in name. The first major crisis Basil II encountered was when Bulgarian Tsar Samuel invaded the Byzantine territory and captured the city of Larissa, the capital of the province of Thessaly (modern Larissa, Greece). In 986, Basil led his forces through the mountain pass, known as the Gates of Trajan, to attack Serdica (modern-day Sofia, Bulgaria). After the unsuccessful siege, Basil decided to return the same way. Unfortunately, Tsar Samuel learned about his plans and laid an ambush in the mountain pass. The Bulgarians annihilated the Byzantine army, but Basil managed to escape death.

On another occasion, Basil II influenced the course of Russian history and shaped their religious beliefs. When his rule was challenged in 989 by Bardas Phokas, a Byzantine military general, Basil turned to Prince Vladimir I of Kyiv, asking for help. The prince of Kyiv promised he would send 6,000 men under the condition that Basil gave him his sister Anna in marriage. In turn, the Byzantine emperor said he would allow him to marry his sister only if he converted from his pagan worship of gods to Orthodox Christianity. Vladimir kept his word, and after marrying Anna, he started converting his people on a massive scale.

Even though Basil wanted to concentrate on recovering the empire's cities that had fallen under Bulgarian rule, he had to turn his focus to Syria in 995 and fight the Muslim Arabs, who had taken over Aleppo. But Basil didn't only save this one city. He continued his campaign in Syria until 1000 CE, recovering much of the territories that had once belonged to the Byzantine Empire.

In 1014, Basil II was able to once again turn to the Bulgarian problem. The culmination of the struggles between the Byzantine Empire and the Bulgarian Empire erupted in the Battle of Kleidion, with Basil II's and Tsar Samuel's forces finally clashing in a decisive conflict. It was at this point that Basil earned his nickname the "Bulgar Slayer," as he led his forces to victory. Although the battle belonged to the Byzantines, Samuel managed to escape. Nevertheless, Basil captured over 15,000 enemy soldiers. He blinded every 99 men out of 100. Those who were left with their eyes were ordered to lead their comrades back to their tsar. The story goes that Samuel died shortly after seeing his soldiers mutilated, apparently of shock. The fight with the Bulgarians continued until 1018 when they finally submitted to the Byzantine Empire.

The rule of Basil II is considered to be the peak of the Byzantine Empire in the Middle Ages. Even though Basil proved to be a distinctive military commander and able administrator of the empire, he left no heir. This would prove to be fatal, for it was partly due to this that the Byzantine Empire started its decline. Constantinople became the most important and richest city in Europe during the 10th and 11th centuries, housing more than 400,000 people. The successful administration of the city and the empire also opened many new opportunities for trade with the Western kingdoms. The Byzantine Empire was crucial for the survival of the Silk Road in the Middle Ages, both by exporting and importing various goods. The city itself acted as a mediator in trade between the Far East and the Western kingdoms, which formed the Holy Roman Empire in the 9th century. The goods from the Byzantine Empire were transported to the courts of Britain and even Scotland and Ireland.

But the focus of the emperors in Constantinople always lay in Eastern Europe. There,

instead of trade goods, Byzantium sent their ideology, shaping many new nations'

religious views. Today, one can see the cultural and religious influence the Byzantine Empire had on the Serbs, Bulgarians, and Russians. During the reign of the Macedonian dynasty, the ideology Constantinople supported openly clashed with the religious ideals of Western Europe. This clash would eventually culminate in 1054 with the East-West Schism, also known as the Great Schism.

The Schism

The Great Schism was the final separation of the Christian Church into the Eastern Orthodox Church and the western

Catholic Church. The political disputes between the pope and the Byzantine emperor led to the separation of lands and the proclamation of Frankish kings and later German kings as the protectors of Rome. However, this political divide between West and East not only influenced the territorial integrity of the Roman Empire, but it also had religious implications. This religious conflict, which was going on in the background for centuries, finally culminated in 1054. But when did it start? Scholars can't pinpoint a date when the first conflict between the religious representatives of the East and West began. It may have started as early as the 2nd century when Pope Victor I started the ecclesiastical controversy known as Quartodecimanism. This early conflict in Christianity occurred over the date of the Easter celebration. But if this helped lead to the schism of 1054 is uncertain.

There were many conflicts like Quartodecimanism in the early history of the Christian Church. Each time a minor schism occurred during the 4th, 5th, and later during the 9th century, the Church remained whole, even though it produced various leaders within its fold. Probably the most important minor schisms were the Acacian and Photian schisms. The first one occurred in 484, and it lasted until 519. Pope Felix III excommunicated Patriarch Acacius of Constantinople for taking Eastern Christianity closer to miaphysitism (a doctrine that defines the nature of Christ semantically different from what was established at the Council of Chalcedon in 451). The Photian Schism occurred in 863, and it lasted for four years. The main issue between Rome and Constantinople was whether the emperor had the right to appoint a new patriarch without the pope's approval.

The pope of Rome and the patriarch of Constantinople had many conflicts. This was possibly because Rome was designated as the first above all metropolitan sees during the first ecclesiastical council in 325 (the Council of Nicaea). Rome was followed by Alexandria, Antioch, and other churches of Roman provinces before Constantinople. However, another council occurred in 381, in which Constantinople was raised to the second position of the metropolitan sees. Religious leaders believed that Constantinople should be the main metropolitan city. After all, it was already the capital of the empire and the city of the emperor's residence. But Rome was the original see, and the Eternal City wouldn't allow anyone to forget that. Another council was held in 451 (the Council of Chalcedon), in which it was decided that the Byzantine Empire would be separated into five great sees, each one overseeing a certain territory. Thus, five patriarchs were chosen, and their importance in order was the patriarch of Rome, of Constantinople, of Alexandria, of Antioch, and of Jerusalem. But Pope Leo I had a problem with the designated territories. He mainly complained that the newly acquired territories of Pontus and Thrace should get their own patriarchy, with its base at Nicaea. This issue would remain a cause of many conflicts between Rome and Constantinople up until the final division in 1054.

By 661, Muslims had taken over some of the territories that belonged to the Patriarchies of Alexandria, Antioch, and Jerusalem. These territories would never be retrieved, and the two main patriarchies left within the Byzantine Empire were Rome and Constantinople. It was only natural for the two great sees to enter into a conflict for supremacy. An argument erupted in 867, and it would continue to dominate the religious scene for the next twelve years. In that time, three new councils would be held to decide whether the supremacy belonged to the West or the East. Up until now, the text of the Nicene Creed, which had been established in 325, claimed the Holy Spirit proceeds "from the father." Rome wanted to add "and from the Son" (Latin: *Filioque*), but the Eastern Church declined. The patriarch of Constantinople went so far as to excommunicate the pope, creating an even deeper schism between the two sees. After this dispute, each see held its own "Fourth Council of Constantinople," with each see recognizing only its council and denouncing the other one.

All these conflicts were just a prelude to what was to come in 1054. The final conflict that would set the destiny of the Eastern and Western Churches started a year earlier when Leo of Ohrid, Archbishop of Bulgaria, wrote a letter to John, Bishop of Trani, complaining about the practices of the Western Church, such as using unleavened bread (unfermented bread) during their rites. He also complained about how the Western bishops, including the pope himself, practiced different fasting customs than those proscribed in Constantinople. At the same time, in Constantinople, Patriarch Michael I Cerularius raised similar issues with Pope Leo IX, but he also complained about the previously disputed filioque clause and about the pope's efforts to assert his authority over the see of Constantinople.

In his defense, Pope Leo IX replied to Cerularius, citing the *Donation of Constantine*, a forged document in which Constantine the Great supposedly donated Rome and the whole western part of the Roman Empire to the pope. This document was probably composed later, most likely during the 8th century, for unknown reasons. However, various popes used this document to prove that the papacy had political authority over the western territories of the empire. Even during the 13th century, the pope would continue using this document to assert his authority over Italy. But Leo IX didn't convince the patriarch of Constantinople that the falsified document was genuine and that the pope had the supremacy over the Christian Church. Instead, Cerularius reacted by refusing to admit papal legates and discussing the matter further with them.

But the conflict between the Eastern and Western Christian Church had to be put aside for the moment, as the Norman conquest threatened both papal and Byzantine possessions in southern Italy. The Normans were an ethnic group of people from northern France (Normandy), and they were a mixture of the Franks and the Vikings. Their attack on southern Italy was due to the invitation of Prince Guaimar III of Salerno, who needed knights to defend his country from the invading Saracens (Arab Muslims). However, the defenders turned into invaders in 999 and started spreading through the southern Italian Peninsula. Finally, around 1054, they became a serious threat to Byzantine and the papal territories, and the two were forced to seek each other's help. Emperor Constantine IX Monomachos and Cerularius wrote letters to the pope, hoping to appease the conflict, but in his reply, Leo IX demanded Rome's supremacy over Constantinople.

In April 1054, Pope Leo IX died. His cardinals, the legates in Constantinople, insisted on discussing the various issues of the Church with the patriarch, even though the death of the pope left them without legitimacy. When Cerularius refused to see them again on July 16th, 1054, they fabricated an edict that stated the patriarch was excommunicated. They even added the names of Leo of Ohrid and all of their followers who joined them in their complaints against the practices of the Western Church.

The patriarch of Constantinople finally reacted, and he gathered a synod on July 20th, with more than twenty bishops taking part. Together, they excommunicated the papal legates, but this did not include their followers or the whole Western Church. The same day, all the Roman churches in Constantinople were closed. It is quite interesting that, at the time, contemporary historians and writers didn't think much of this event. This wasn't the first schism between the East and West, and since the others were settled relatively fast, they believed this one would be too. However, the East and West never again reconciled, and the Church has remained divided since.

The two parts of the Christian Church were also ignorant of how deep this schism would influence them. Through the next few centuries, relations between them would remain friendly. Because of this, the schism between East and West is not observed as a single event. It was a series of disagreements that led the two parts of the same Church to further develop in different directions. The divide probably became obvious during the Crusades when the Catholic knights sacked Constantinople and converted some of its populace. They also took some of the holy relics and gifted them to their Catholic churches in the West.

Back in Rome

After the Great Schism of 1054, Rome started quickly rising to prominence. It was the center of the Catholic Church and the center of papal power over the Papal States. At this point in history, the pope was constantly in conflict with the rulers of the Western European kingdoms, as the power struggle over supremacy erupted. The pope was a religious leader, but as such, he wanted ultimate authority over the kings. On the other hand, the kings always strived to separate the ecclesiastical from the secular. Some even thought the king should have the power to dictate his kingdom's religion. Besides the Western kings, the pope was also in conflict with the Roman citizens, who were in dire need of a secular ruler. This conflict resulted in the pope's exile from the city, which lasted for almost half a century.

During the early 11th century, right after the Great Schism, Rome was reemerging as a cultural and economic center. The city was buzzing with life, with various merchants, artists, artisans, and pilgrims walking the streets. This was also the period when other Italian cities, such as Genoa and Venice, started developing their trade across the Mediterranean Sea. This trade brought the cities wealth, and with wealth came the desire for independence. The rich merchant class quickly replaced the old aristocratic families who once ruled the cities, and these northern Italian cities became more and more autonomous, even though they were still part of the Holy Roman Empire.

The citizens of Rome were well aware of the situation in other cities, and they wanted similar freedoms. Soon, a rebellion formed in 1144, in which the people demanded the pope loosen the grip he had on the city. They also wanted to get rid of the ruling noble class.

One Roman citizen stood out as the leader of the rebellion: Giordano Pierleoni. He was the son of the consul and the head of a major banking family in Rome. He led the rebellion against the pope's power and against the aristocracy, who wouldn't abide by the new ideas of establishing the Roman government based on the principles of the old Roman Republic. When the rebels took over the city, they expelled Pope Lucius II and established the Commune of Rome.

The Roman Commune looked up to the ancient Roman Republic, and the people organized a senate that had full authority over the city. They first met in 1144, where they elected the leader of the rebellion, Giordano Pierleoni, as the first patrician of Rome. The senate had fifty-six senators. Each district of medieval Rome sent four representatives as senators, and there were fourteen districts in total. Pope Lucius II gathered his supporters and attacked Rome in the hopes he would be able to take it back from the people, but his efforts failed. Pierleoni was quick to set up the city defenses, and when the battle arrived in 1154, Pope Lucius II was hit in the head with a stone. He failed to retake the city, and immediately after the battle, he died of the head wound.

The new pope, Eugene III, led negotiations with the Roman Commune and was allowed to return to the city in 1152. The negotiations did not lead to the end of the Roman Commune, but the senators realized they needed the support of the Holy Roman Empire if the city was to survive in the cruel world of the Middle Ages. To gain this, the senate decided to allow the pope to return to Rome. However, from this point on, the Roman Commune would often find itself between the conflicting pope and the Holy Roman Empire.

The Roman Commune's government wasn't recognized until 1188 when Pope Clement III finally succumbed to their pleas. With this recognition came the end to the conflict between the city and the pope. The Roman people were finally free to elect their own magistrates, and the city gained its autonomy, even though it remained a vassal to the Papal States. In 1193, the Roman Commune ended when the senate was reduced to only one senator. With a reduced senate, it was easy for the pope to take over the authority of the city once more. Even though the rebellions continued, Rome was never again free of the pope's grip until Italy united during the 19th century.

The same struggles occurred in the 13th century when aristocratic families fought the pope, as they wanted to take control over the city. Guelphs and Ghibellines were the names of the two factions, with the first supporting the pope and the second supporting his rivals, which ranged from aristocratic families to Holy Roman emperors. This rivalry may have started as a struggle for control over Rome, but it soon turned into a struggle for power over the Holy Roman Empire. The conflicts were many and often, and they lasted until the 15th century. It was during the early conflicts of Guelphs and Ghibellines, in 1277, that the pope's seat was moved from the Lateran Palace (southeast Rome) to the Vatican.

During the 12th and 13th centuries, the pope was at the peak of his rule over the secular matters of the Holy Roman Empire. It was during the Crusades that the pope had a leading role in religion, as well as in everyday life, politics, and economy of not only the Papal States but also the whole empire. After all, the Crusades were a series of holy wars, and as such, they could only be administered by the pope himself. The kings, emperors, and the aristocracy of the West were nothing but the pope's servants, who fulfilled their duty by leading an army to the Holy Land (Near East), where they fought with the Muslims for the control over territories and religious freedoms.

But during the 14th century, Western rulers realized they had lost control over their kingdoms while being away on the Crusades. In 1302, Pope Boniface VIII declared that all living souls should be subjected to the papal rule. The King of France, Philip IV, objected. In return, the pope excommunicated the French ruler and wanted to put a religious interdict over his kingdom, which would prevent its citizens from performing religious rituals. But before he could achieve this, he was attacked and beaten to death by Philip's allies in Rome. King Philip intervened in the elections for the new pope, and soon, his friend was elevated to the office, taking the name Pope Clement V. After this instance, the next six popes would all be of French origin, and the French influence in the papacy was evident.

In 1305, the Holy See of Rome was transferred to Poitiers (western France) and then again in 1309 to Avignon (southeastern France). The pope had to flee Rome because the Roman citizens and the aristocratic families of previous popes strongly opposed the French influence. Avignon proved to be a perfect haven, as it was surrounded by the Comtat Venaissin, a Papal State. The proximity of the French king and his army also played a major role in the choice of a new residency for the pope, but it also brought some innovations to the ecclesiastical see. It transformed from being primarily a church to a papal court. The lifestyle of the clerks became similar to the lifestyle of the courtiers of European kingdoms. Intrigue and conspiracy, as well as nepotism, were common occurrences, but at least the French-influenced popes admitted that secular power was no longer in their hands.

Seven popes resided in Avignon before the pope's residency returned to Rome. The decision to move again was brought up by Pope Gregory XI in 1376, but it would take him almost a full year to fulfill his plan. He, too, was born in France and was elected with the support of the French king, but his decision had nothing to do with this. Instead, he feared the prolonged conflict between the Guelphs and Ghibellines would rid him of Rome's allegiance. To prohibit that, the pope needed to return to the Eternal City and take the matter into his own hands. Before he decided to return to Rome, the pope put an embargo on the grain import into the cities of the Italian Peninsula, which were predominantly inhabited by his opposers, the Ghibellines. These cities were Bologna, Milan, Genoa, Lucca, and Perugia. In response to the pope's embargo, the cities rose in rebellion. To quell this uprising, the Guelphs decided to hire Breton mercenaries. Unfortunately, a massacre started, and more than 2,500 people lost their lives. The massacre only further angered the hungry people of the Italian cities, and the opposition to the pope strengthened further, threatening to claim Rome itself.

When Pope Gregory XI returned to Rome on January 17th, 1377, he didn't have time to set up his court or enjoy his new residence, as he soon died. His successor was Pope Urban VI, who was born in Rome. He immediately got rid of the French influence and the French cardinals who had followed Gregory from Avignon. Angered, these cardinals held their own elections for the pope's successor and chose Clement VII. This animosity between the Romans and the French cardinals continued until the 15th century, with each faction electing their head of the Roman Catholic Church (known as the Papal Schism). But the ecumenical Council of Constance, which lasted for four years, from 1414 to 1418, finally resolved this issue, proclaiming the French elections as illegitimate.

In the East, turbulent times were brewing while the pope's see was in Avignon. The power struggle for the succession of the throne in Constantinople led to a civil war, in which the growing Ottoman Empire got involved. After that, the Ottomans desired the city of Constantinople and other Byzantine territories for themselves. In 1366, Emperor John V Palaiologos embarked on a tour across Europe in search of help against the rising Ottomans. In October of 1367, he even reached Rome, where he asked Pope Urban V, who was only visiting the city as the see was in Avignon, for help. In the hopes he would end the Great Schism and bring about a new alliance between the Byzantine Empire and the Holy Roman Empire, John converted to Catholicism. But the pope denied him any help, and he even condemned the reunification of the Christian

Churches. These events would culminate in the fall of Constantine and the end of the Byzantine Empire.

The Fall of Constantinople

During the first few Crusades, Constantinople was torn apart by the internal struggles for succession. But this wasn't the only struggle in the city. Greek citizens and emperors of Greek descent were against the Crusades, while the Latin citizens and the emperors they supported were pro-Crusades. Various throne claimants needed financial help to hire an army to fight their opponents, and the state as a whole was soon in great debt to the Venetian Republic. In 1204, the leaders of Venice and the Crusaders wanted things settled within the city, and they thought the only way to achieve this would be the conquest of Constantinople and the division of the Byzantine Empire. The city was sacked, and the Crusaders established their own Latin Empire. The Byzantine Empire was split into many smaller successor states, but this wasn't permanent. In 1261, the Byzantine Empire was retrieved by the Byzantines under the new rulership of the Palaiologos dynasty. However, the empire was already weakened, and it would never achieve its previous glory again.

The neighboring kingdoms quickly realized the Byzantine Empire was still unstable. The Latins, Bulgarians, Serbs, and Ottomans constantly tried to bring it down, yet Byzantium persisted. The Ottoman Empire rose to power at this time and started conquering some of the Byzantine possessions in their vicinity. Constantinople and the Byzantine Empire were further weakened by the Black Death (1346–1349) and the economic decline the disease brought. The attack on Byzantium continued, and the empire was no more than the city of Constantinople and its surrounding territories by the mid-15th century.

In 1451, nineteen-year-old Mehmed II succeeded his father on the Ottoman throne. No one saw him as a threat, even though he immediately started construction of a fortress (RUMELIHISARI), which would give him full control over the Bosporus. Mehmed II's fortress was right across from the older one, which had been built by his predecessor, Bayezid I. The two fortresses, one on the European and the other one on the Asian side, were perfect starting points for the expansion of the Ottoman Empire into Europe. The only one who realized the intentions of the young sultan was Emperor Constantine XI of Constantinople, who immediately asked the European kingdoms for help.

The Balkans were endangered, but the Ottomans first had to pass Constantinople to gain access to the rest of Europe. Constantine XI believed his Western counterparts realized that, and he especially begged the Western Church and Pope Nicholas V for assistance. But just like his predecessor, John V Palaiologos, Constantine was declined. The Great Schism of 1054 hadn't been forgotten, and both the Roman pope in Rome and the Constantinople patriarch couldn't agree that peace was necessary. This religious conflict had already sealed the Balkans' fate.

However, there were some good intentions in Rome for the reunification of the Churches. Pope Nicholas changed his mind and sent Cardinal Isidore, former Metropolitan of Kiev (Kyiv), to Constantinople to negotiate the possibility of a reunion. The cardinal brought along around 200 archers from Naples in case he needed extra defense to escape the city. The service took place on December 12th, 1452, in Hagia Sophia. The union was signed, and the pope promised he would persuade the Western kings to come to Constantinople's side when the time was right. However, the Western kingdoms had troubles of their own and were in no shape to send military aid. England and France needed time to recover from their 100-year war, and Spain just finished fighting the Reconquista. The Holy Roman Empire had its internal struggles, while Hungary and Poland were fighting a war of their own with the Ottomans.

The pope sent several troops he managed to gather from the Papal States, but this was not enough for the defense of Constantinople. Genoa didn't officially send help, but some of its people decided to help defend Byzantium. They even brought Johannes Grant, an engineer, with them. He came up with the idea of counter-mining tunnels to prevent the invaders from entering Constantinople beneath its walls.

It was Easter Monday, April 2ⁿᵈ, 1453, when Mehmet I's army showed up in front of Constantinople's walls. The city gates were closed at the first sight of the enemy, and the siege began. The first offer Emperor Constantine IX received came on April 6ᵗʰ, in which Mehmed was willing to allow him and his citizens to surrender without casualties. The Byzantines declined, as they weren't willing to bow down to Muslim rulers. The artillery bombardment of the city then began. Mehmet had the help of the Hungarian engineer Orban (also known as Urban), who constructed the famous cannon that brought down the walls of Constantinople. At first, Orban offered his services to Constantine, but since the Byzantine emperor couldn't pay the asked price, Orban sent the offer to Mehmet.

The siege of Constantinople prolonged beyond what Mehmet had planned. He relied on the numbers of his army and the high ground he occupied outside of the city walls. However, the Byzantine emperor was persistent, and he wisely used all the help he had managed to gather. The Venetians came to support the naval battles, but they were greatly outnumbered. Nevertheless, they showed their loyalty when they returned to the city after their scouting mission, risking their own lives. The Genoese tirelessly worked on repairing the city walls where Orban's cannon had managed to breach.

It was day fifty-three of the siege, Tuesday, May 29ᵗʰ, when Mehmet ordered the decisive attack. The day before, Christians from the Ottoman army sent arrows with messages attached to them across the city walls. They warned the emperor of the upcoming attack, but it was too late for Constantine to do anything. Sultan Mehmet I sent wave after wave of attackers on the city, targeting the spot where the River Lycus ran into the city. That was its weakest point, but the defenders managed to sustain four attacks. Unfortunately, by that point, the Genoese leader, Giovanni Giustiniani, was injured, and his men abandoned their posts to carry him to a medic. This allowed the Ottomans to breach the outer wall and start their attack on the inner one.

The morale of the defenders went down, and not long after, the first Ottomans climbed the city walls and raised their flag. They also discovered the small door, known as the Kerkoporta, was left open, and suddenly, the enemy swarmed the city. The city fell, and the Ottomans started slaughtering, raping, and pillaging the city. Their ferocity was such that even their sultan was disgusted, and he called them all off after less than a day. Finally, Mehmet was able to enter the city and proclaim himself as the victor.

The taking of the great city wasn't simply a matter of conquest for the sultan. If he allowed Constantinople to thrive, the Byzantine Empire would eventually try to spread its dominion over Ottoman territories. For Mehmet, taking Constantinople was a matter of defense, but it also gave him the opportunity to strengthen his empire. From there, the Ottomans would launch their conquest of Europe, which would last for the next six centuries. However, they would only manage to take the Balkans. At their peak, the Ottomans would reach the city walls of Vienna, but they weren't successful in taking it. As for Constantinople, it never ceased to exist. It became the capital of the Ottoman Empire, and it was renamed Istanbul. Today, the city of Constantine the Great is the capital of modern-day Turkey.

Chapter 9 – The Renaissance

The Renaissance in Europe is generally described as starting in the 14th century and lasting until the 17th. However, the starting point of the Renaissance is still disputed. Some claim that the first traces of humanism (which is integral to the Renaissance) can be seen in paintings from the early 13th century, but most argue that the true Renaissance came in the middle of the 15th century. Whenever it occurred, the Renaissance originated in Italy, and Rome was in a perfect position to be influenced. The center of the movement was Florence, and from there, it easily spread through the rest of Europe.

The Renaissance influenced all aspects of life: art, philosophy, science, literature, politics, and the economy. It inspired many individuals, who gave us some of the most extraordinary paintings, music, and ideas. But it also inspired traveling and discovering the unknown world. New cultures were integrated into what was then a modern society, but most of the Renaissance was about rediscovering classical history. During the Middle Ages, humanity mostly forgot its past, and Rome, Athens, and Alexandria, although still thriving cities, hid their past under the covers of religion. This is precisely why medieval times are often referred to as the Dark Ages today. The fall of Constantinople brought many Greek refugees to the West, who carried many texts and arts that had been forgotten. With them came the renewed interest in humanity's past.

During the Renaissance, a cultural movement known as humanism began. It is tightly bound to the Renaissance because it was born out of it. Once people started discovering their past, they learned much about themselves. This moved the focus point from religion and God to humanity. Man was suddenly the center of his universe, and he started embracing humanity's achievements, education, art, and science. Medicine was no longer a miracle anymore; it was the endeavor of science and hard work. Art was not a divine inspiration anymore; it originated in the human mind. And what humans they were. The Renaissance gave the world individuals such as Leonardo da Vinci, Desiderius Erasmus, Galileo, Copernicus, Niccolò Machiavelli, Titian, John Milton, William Shakespeare, and Sandro Botticelli.

The Renaissance Popes

When the pope moved his see from Rome to Avignon, the city was already dying. At the time, Rome wasn't a commercial or trade center. Its income largely depended on pilgrims who would come to see the pope, and he was no longer there. The city that had over a million inhabitants in the 1st century CE now had slightly over 25,000 at the beginning of the 15th century. The city degraded, and just when it seemed there was no chance of returning Rome's old glory, the pope decided to return.

After the Papal Schism, which occurred between 1414 and 1418, a new pope was elected. He took the name Pope Martin V. After the Council of Constance, the new pope decided to travel around Italy instead of immediately going to Rome. He lingered in Florence, where the Renaissance was already taking over. He entered Rome in 1420, and he brought the new ideas he had admired in Florence with him. Pope Martin V immediately started rebuilding the Eternal City, its palaces, churches, bridges, and all the other public structures. But he was only one man, and it would take a whole century for Rome to reach the peak of its Renaissance, which happened under the careful eye of the papacy. To gather enough money for the development of the city, the future popes would have to sell church offices and implement heavy taxes on the Papal States. This would eventually lead to many of the states desiring the end of the pope's authority over them. However, the Church had a tight grip on the territories. The destiny of Rome and the Papal States would constantly be intertwined with that of the Church.

Pope Martin V wasn't the only pope who found inspiration for rebuilding Rome in Florence. His successor, Pope Eugene IV, was met with resistance and open rebellion early in his papacy in 1434. He was forced to escape the city, and he found a haven in Florence. There, he was inspired by the buildings and literary activity, which was at its peak. At that time, Florence Cathedral had just been finished, and the new pope marveled at its glory. He wanted one just like that in Rome. Unfortunately, Pope Eugene did not have sufficient funding for such a grand project, but he could at least finance the construction of new bronze doors for the already existing St. Peter's Basilica. The doors were marvelous, showing Jesus, Mary, St. Peter, and Pope Eugene IV.

At this point, Pope Eugene ordered a new design for the whole city of Rome, and an architect, named Leon Battista Alberti, proposed his plan for the geometric arrangement of the city, with its center on the Capitoline Hill. Unfortunately, Pope Eugene didn't live long enough to see his city rebuilt. However, Alberti became the personal architect of the next pope, Nicholas V. This was the pope who lived through turbulent events that shook Europe, such as the end of the Hundred Years' War and the fall of Constantinople. But Pope Nicholas isn't remembered only for that. It was his papacy that brought recognition to Rome for its successes and achievements in politics, science, and literature. Nicholas V was inspired by humanism, and he realized that a new diplomatic approach was needed to repair the relations between Rome and the Holy Roman Empire. At the congress in Lodi, a treaty was achieved that brought peace to the cities of Milan, Naples, and Florence, which had warred against each other. Nicholas V also brought peace to the Roman papacy by establishing good relations with Charles VII of France (who still wanted the Avignon papacy).

Pope Nicholas V was also the first to think about Rome's cleanliness. Instead of only rebuilding the streets, he also gave careful thought to restoring the water supply and the construction of canals, which would take away the dirt from the city. Nicolas was the first person to think about restoring the aqueducts of ancient Rome, which had been destroyed in the 6th century by the barbarian invaders. As for the churches, he rebuilt many of them, all Roman Catholic churches. He carefully planned new business and residential quarters to be built in the vicinity of the Ponte Sant'Angelo bridge. Nicolas V was only the pope for eight years, and all the work he began couldn't be finished in that short period.

His successor, Pope Sixtus IV (1471–1484), continued much of the work commissioned in previous years. However, he is most famous for commissioning the Sistine Chapel, which was even named after him (the original name was *Cappella Magna*, "Great Chapel"). He employed a Florentine artist named Michelangelo Buonarroti to paint its ceiling with its famous scene *The Creation of Adam*, which stands even today to testify the greatness of the two men, the pope and the painter. Rome transformed from a ruined, barely habited city to a large construction site that attracted many famous architects and artists willing to contribute to its greatness. Soon, the city of Rome was able to dazzle even the great northern cities with its beauty and richness.

But with the shine of the rich and famous came the decadent life of its rulers. The Spanish House of Borgia came to power when Alexander VI was elected as the successor to the papacy. The Borgia's intrigues and power plays are known worldwide, and they inspire many stories, movies, and plays to this day. Pope Alexander VI was controversial and, at the same time, had a conflicting persona. He is known for his many scandals, such as openly endorsing the children he had with various mistresses, nepotism, and enjoying a lavish lifestyle filled with many sins. But he was also described as the best pope ever to be elected, at least by his contemporaries.

Besides the various intrigues, Pope Alexander VI was also remembered for his involvement in the Italian Wars (1494-1559). These wars erupted in Renaissance Italy because the major European powers wanted control over the independent states of the Italian Peninsula. Some of the independent states, such as the Republic of Naples, the Republic of Venice, and the Duchy of Milan, were in constant search for powerful allies to start their expansionist efforts. But the European powers saw these alliances as possibilities to assert their own dominion over Italy. The most important among them were France, the Holy Roman Empire, and Spain.

The wars began with Charles VIII's invasion of Italy in 1494. He immediately managed to seize Naples. However, Spain and the Holy Roman Empire made a coalition with Pope Alexander VI, Venice, and Milan to expel the French. They were successful, but in 1499, the successor of Charles VIII, Louis XII, returned. He occupied Milan and Genoa and was preparing to attack Naples. For this endeavor, he gained the consent of the Spanish King Ferdinand II and even of the pope. But the problem escalated when the question of territorial division was brought up. It culminated in open warfare between France and Spain in 1502. In 1504, the Treaty of Blois was signed, in which France gained control over Milan and Genoa, while Naples was given to Spain.

New troubles began in 1508 when Pope Julius II allied with France, Spain, and the Holy Roman Empire against the Republic of Venice. This alliance was known as the League of Cambrai, and its task was to check the territorial expansion of Venice. French military troops were victorious against the Venetians at the Battle of Agnadello in 1509. Shortly after, the pope allied with Venice to expel the French from their territory. He started forming the Holy League in 1510. The main members of this league were the Swiss cantons, Ferdinand II of Aragon, Henry VIII of England, and Holy Roman Emperor Maximilian I. The Swiss army was successful at routing the French at Novara, but the death of Pope Julius II in 1513 ended the Holy League. Two years later, the French proclaimed victory and reestablished their authority over Lombardy.

The war was again reignited when the rivalry between Francis I of France and Charles V of Spain (who was also the Holy Roman emperor) erupted. In the Battle of Pavia in 1525, the French were beaten, and their king was forced to sign the Treaty of Madrid. With this treaty, France gave up all of its Italian possessions, as well as Burgundy. But soon, Francis I refused to acknowledge this treaty, and he forced a new league with Pope Clement VII, Henry VIII of England, and the Republics of Venice and Florence. Charles V wanted to punish the pope for his involvement, and he sent French Charles III, Duke of Bourbon, to Rome. He led an army of over 20,000 men, and in 1527, they successfully invaded the city. Their sack of Rome lasted for a full week. The war ended with a new treaty, which was signed in Cambrai (France) in 1529. Again, the French king had to renounce his claims in Italy. Two more wars followed in which Francis I tried to gain back his authority over Italy. Both of them were failures, and King Francis died in 1547 after the treaty of Crépy, in which he resigned Naples for the third time. Spain managed to assert its dominance throughout Italy under the rule of Philip II. The Italian Wars left Italy in ruins, and soon, chivalry was abandoned as a virtue among the knights. But some good came out of the warfare. The parties involved had to cross all of Europe to move their troops to Italy and back to their respective kingdoms. By doing this, each soldier brought a piece of the Italian

Renaissance home with him. The philosophy of humanism, the Renaissance arts, and political and economic ideas were spreading through Europe like wildfire.

The popes were also patrons of the arts and science, which is understandable since their idea was to attract artists and engineers who could work on rebuilding Rome. But they didn't focus only on building projects. Their idea for Rome was for it to be just as glorious, if not more, as the northern cities, such as Florence, Milan, and Venice. For this, the popes needed painters, sculptors, and musicians to work at their court, as well as literary masters who would witness it all and write about it so they could leave evidence of Rome's glory for future generations. Pope Nicholas V even brought some of the most eminent scientists of the time to Rome. One of them was Lorenzo Valla, a humanist and scholar, who proved that the document *Donation of Constantine* is a forgery. Another great scholar was Vespasiano da Bisticci. He helped Pope Nicholas V establish the Vatican Library, although the building would be constructed later, during the time of Sixtus IV. The library was officially opened in 1471.

The term "Renaissance man" is something we use today to describe a polymath, a person whose expertise is not limited only to one area but who knows many subjects. This polymath would use his vast knowledge to solve elaborate and complex problems. A Renaissance man never limited himself just to poetry, science, or architecture. Instead, he would gather many abilities and use them to serve humanity. One of the best examples of a Renaissance man is Leon Battista Alberti. He was an architect, author, poet, priest, linguist, cryptographer, philosopher, and an engineer. Besides his intellectual skills, Leon Battista Alberti was a successful athlete and horse rider. In 1431, he stepped into the papal service by taking the holy orders (a right one must pass to become a priest). He was most interested in studying old Roman ruins, which gave him inspiration for his architectural work. This was precisely why Pope Nicholas V employed him to work on the restoration of an aqueduct, now known as Acqua Vergine.

The successors of Pope Nicholas V, Callixtus III and Pius II, brought a man named Flavio Biondo into their service in 1433. This man is known as the father of early archaeology. He was the first man to study the ancient ruins of Rome, and he even published a three-tome encyclopedia that detailed the topography of ancient Rome. He was friends with Leon Battista Alberti, and together, they explored the forgotten and overgrown ruins of the city. At the time, ancient Rome was already buried underground, so before Flavio could approach it, he had to dig it out.

Chapter 10 – Modern History of Rome

Early Modern History

The modern history of Rome started with a religious scandal when Martin Luther accused the pope and the Roman Catholic Church of greed and started the Reformation movement. This movement resulted in the separation of the Catholic Church and Protestantism. German and English Protestant sects formed, and they continued to challenge the prestige of Rome and the pope's authority. To save the situation and the integrity of the Catholic Church, Pope Paul III gathered an ecumenical council in Trent in 1545. This council was effective until 1563, and its main purpose was to fight the Protestant Reformation.

The elaborate work of the ecumenical council is known as the Counter-Reformation, during which the Catholic Church brought several decisions that still resonate in the world. Some important decisions were the adoption of the Gregorian calendar and the first Jesuit missions to China and Japan. They also founded the Gregorian University in Rome, where young students prepared to become priests. Besides theology, this university taught natural sciences, such as mathematics and astronomy. At the same time, the

Catholic Church condemned some of the greatest minds of early modern history with its newly founded Roman Inquisition.

In 1593, Giordano Bruno was held captive in Rome for his theories that the universe was infinite and that the Earth could not possibly be its center. He dared to ask the question of how one can find the center in an infinite space. His other theories involved the thought of stars as distant suns with their own planets that could hold life. For this, Giordano Bruno was charged with blasphemy and heresy, and he was tried for seven years. During that time, he was a prisoner of the pope, who asked him to renounce his philosophy in favor of Catholic dogma. Bruno said he had never abandoned his belief in religious dogmas, but he also continued to defend his thesis of the plurality of worlds. The scientist was found guilty, and for his crimes, he was burned at the stake in 1600. Giordano Bruno wasn't the only scientist who suffered the judgment of the Roman Inquisition. In 1633, Galileo Galilei, the father of modern physics, was tried for his theses and theories. Galileo was placed under house arrest, where he died in 1642.

With the Counter-Reformation came the reformation of the papal court. The Renaissance popes were known to enjoy the splendor of the court, indulging in many sins in the process. This was why they were accused of greed by Martin Luther in the first place. If they wanted to preserve the authority of the Roman Catholic Church, the popes had to give up their nepotism, corruption, mistresses, and parties. Strangely enough, the Catholic Church clean-up reforms were instigated by Pope Pius IV, who was notorious for his nepotism. He employed his nephew, Charles Borromeo, to run the reforms. During this period, the papal court was cleansed of all pomp, such as musicians and jokers. Any member of the court caught in blasphemy or with a mistress would be severely punished. All prostitutes were exiled from Rome; however, if they had special permission, they would be confined to specific districts. The Roman Inquisition was implemented throughout the city, and the pope's palace was renovated so it could accommodate even more prisoners.

Prostitutes were not the only ones to be confined within the city's districts. During Pope Paul IV, Rome established a ghetto, in which Jews were placed. This compound was walled off from the city. The gates of the ghetto were locked during the night, while during the day, the Jews were free to leave. However, they had to wear a certain mark, like during Nazi Germany, by which they would be recognized. For men, this was a yellow hat, while women wore a yellow scarf. Life in the ghetto was poor. Even though Jews were allowed to be pawnbrokers, the Christians resented them so much that no one would approach them for business. Although they were officially allowed to practice their religion, Jews were forced to listen to a Christian sermon every Saturday. The Jews in the confined area of the city multiplied, and soon, there was no room for all of them. Since they were not allowed to expand the ghetto, they were forced to build their homes vertically, which blocked the sun. Overcrowding and poverty led to many diseases inside the ghetto. During 1656, the plague entered Rome, and the Jewish ghetto was hit the hardest due to bad hygienic conditions. Around 800 Jews died. This number might seem low, but at the time, there were around 4,000 Jews in Rome.

The popes of Rome reached the peak of power in the 18th century. The Papal States expanded their territory to include Romagna in the north and the enclaves of Pontecorvo and Benevento to the south. The pope was still in charge of the Comtat Venaissin, which surrounded Avignon. These were the times when the Baroque and Rococo styles reigned, which brought new architecture to the buildings of Rome, such as the famous Trevi Fountain. Eighteenth-century Rome also saw the opening of the world's first museum, the Palazzo Nuovo (1734). The first tourists arrived in Rome and were recognized as such instead of as pilgrims.

The 18th century was also the period when the Society of Jesus, most commonly known as the Jesuits, thrived in Rome. They were a religious order with a mission to spread Christianity beyond the borders of Europe. Even though the order was founded in the 16th century, it was during the 18th century that they had the strongest support of the pope, allowing them to spread their influence more vigorously through North America.

Italy Unified

When the First Coalition (the Holy Roman Empire, Spain, Prussia, etc.) was organized to fight the Kingdom of France (and later the Republic of France) during the Revolutionary Wars, Napoleon Bonaparte planned to take the fighting to Italy and occupy it. At the time, the pope and the Papal States were a part of the First Coalition, but they were unsuccessful in defending northern Italy. After Napoleon concluded his campaign there, he turned his focus to the south and Rome. The invasion occurred in February 1798 when all the Papal States were occupied. Pope Pius VI was exiled to France, and Rome became a republic, a vassal state to the Republic of France.

But this French-organized republic wasn't popular among the Italian people. Instead, the war was renewed, and in 1799, Rome was liberated. The Papal States were restored under the authority of Pope Pius VII in 1800. But the peace didn't last for long. The French invaded Rome again in 1808, and the Papal States were now divided between the Republic of France and the Kingdom of Italy. The Papal States were a hotspot for the conflict for the next several decades, and even a triumvirate returned at one point. In1849, Rome became a republic once more, though it was short-lived. Carlo Armellini, Giuseppe Mazzini, and Aurelio Saffi formed a triumvirate to govern the republic. They wanted to allow the pope to continue his governance of the Catholic Church, but he wouldn't be allowed to meddle in secular questions of the Roman Republic. This republic lasted for only one year, as Pope Pius IX soon asked other Catholic states for help, with France responding. Another invasion followed, and the pope was restored with all of his previous powers to govern the Papal States.

In 1861, all of Italy was reunited except for the Papal States. King Victor Emmanuel II was proclaimed the king of Italy. Unified Italy turned its focus toward Rome, as that city had always been a major part of Italian history. Integrating it into the newly founded kingdom would give historical and national identity to the people. This was necessary if Italy was to stay unified. The war between France and Prussia in 1870 was the perfect setting for this to happen. They joined forces with Prussia and gained the excuse to attack the Papal States, which were still under French protection. The Italian army, led by General Raffaele Cadorna, marched into Rome on September 20th, 1870. The pope had no chance of defending the city. He was left with only 13,000 defenders, who were confronted by the Italian army, which numbered over 50,000 men. Rome was not annexed; instead, it joined the Kingdom of Italy. The pope would keep the parts of the city known as the Leonine City and the Vatican, but Pius IX demanded a much broader territory. In return, the Italian government took the whole city and left him with nothing.

Rome became the official capital of Italy the next year, in 1871. The pope had no temporal power, but he remained the head of the Catholic Church. He was free to leave and enter Rome whenever he wanted, but he preferred to stay in his palace and refer to himself as the "prisoner of the Vatican." The nobles who sided with the pope during this dispute became known as the black nobility. They received this nickname because they openly mourned the pope's imprisonment (even though he was not a prisoner). They also claimed to be subjects of the papal state, even though, officially, the state didn't exist yet. The pope would remain in the Vatican for the next fifty-nine years, during which he protested the Italian authority over Rome.

Rome during the Two World Wars

During World War I, Italy tried to remain neutral. However, pressed by outside forces, the government was forced to negotiate with both sides. When the Austrians offered Trentino in exchange for an Italian alliance, the Triple Entente (Britain, France, and Russia) offered not only Trentino but South Tyrol too. They also offered Dalmatia, Istria, Trieste, and Gorizia. The offer was too good to be declined, and in 1915, Italy joined the war, signing the Treaty of London. However, the Italian government signed this treaty in secrecy, as the majority of the political parties and people were against the war. The Socialist Party was against the war, except for Benito Mussolini. He thought the war would be a good way to bring down capitalism and bring forth national liberation. He was swayed by the writings of Karl Marx, who claimed that a social revolution always followed major wars. For his views, Mussolini was expelled from the Socialist Party, but he continued to write pro-war propaganda for his newspapers, *Il Popolo d'Italia* ("The People of Italy").

The First World War was over, and Italy could count its sacrifices. Around 600,000 Italians died on their own soil during the conflict, while 950,000 more were wounded and scarred for life. The people resented the war and the government that had proclaimed it. However, there were also the Nationalists, who defended the idea of war and proudly cheered the Italian victory in the Battle of Vittorio Veneto in 1918. The Kingdom of Italy's flag became a symbol of the division of the people.

After the war, Italy entered a serious economic crisis, and the social revolution appeared imminent. Riots and looting were a common occurrence during the next two years, which are remembered, in modern Italian history, as the Biennio Rosso ("Two Red Years," which took place in 1919 and 1920). The king was obsolete, and the political parties showed their lack of support for the kingdom by leaving the parliament. Strikes happened all over the country, as the workers occupied the factories, demonstrating they could replace the ruling class and produce without their control. The government couldn't do anything but suppress occasional strikes. The whole country was pleading for a revolution.

This post-war political crisis created the perfect atmosphere for a new militant and patriotic movement to rise. In March 1919, journalist Benito Mussolini founded the infamous *Fasci Italiani di Combattimento* (the Italian Fasces of Combat, better known as the Fascists). The main ideas of his league were the confiscation of the war profits, the vote for women, and an eight-hour workday. At first, the Fascists weren't successful in spreading their propaganda, but they steadily grew. The Fascists organized a militia, which started breaking up the strikes, beating the people who supported the Socialists and the Catholics, and overthrowing the local councils. They also often clashed with police and burned down union offices and party newspaper headquarters. Killing was not unusual during their interventions, and many people were even exiled from their cities. By 1921, the Fascists became a major political party supported by the landowners, middle class, and the students. Mussolini became the leader of the party, giving it an official name: the National Fascist Party. He chose Rome as his main city of operations, and in 1922, he organized the "March on Rome," in which he led around 25,000 people to occupy government offices. On October 29th, Mussolini formed his government with himself as the prime minister. During his leadership, the constitutional rule came to an end.

Mussolini gathered enough power to become a dictator, but he didn't join World War II (1939-1945) until 1940. German supremacy over France was evident, and Mussolini thought he could join the Nazis to gain some territory. The first act of Italy in World War II was to cross the Alps and attack France in June 1940. But the very next year came Italy's first military disaster. Italy attacked Greece in 1941, and it was so unsuccessful that Germany had to send its troops to the rescue. In 1942, Italy again needed German help when they tried to take over North Africa. Italy mainly had to thank its poor morale for the military disasters of World War II. The people didn't want to fight for the causes of Nazi Germany, as they were causes they never even believed in. The continuous Allied bombings didn't help either, and Italy lost its ability to produce weapons and food for its army. During the war, the Vatican remained neutral, as Pope Pius XII chose not to meddle. For this, he was scrutinized, as his decision was seen as inaction toward the suffering of the Jewish people. But the Vatican helped Italy change its alliance during the war by providing accurate news. All the people of Italy were subjected to the propaganda material of Prime Minister Mussolini. When the Vatican started its radio broadcast, the truth could finally be heard.

Soon, the Fascist movement could no longer command the obedience of the people. The Grand Council of Rome in July 1943 saw the Fascists officially asking the king to resume his powers, while Mussolini was dismissed from the office of prime minister. On July 25th, King Victor Emmanuel III returned. People all around the country supported this decision, and to show it, they tore down any Fascist symbols and destroyed the statues of Benito Mussolini. Germany didn't like this change, and they started sending their troops to Italy. The new prime minister, Pietro Badoglio, promised he would continue the war, but at the same time, he was negotiating with the Allied Forces. On September 8th, 1943, Italy finally agreed to end all hostilities toward the Allies. Naturally, the alliance with Germany came to an end.

Rome was taken over by the Germans, but in the confusion, the Italian army was left without orders. They didn't know whether to defend the city or to join the Germans. The people resisted and fought their own small guerilla resistance, while the Italian army fled the city, leaving it to the Germans. Only after the fall of Rome did

Badoglio declare war on Germany. For the next eighteen months, the war continued on Italy's territory, with the Allies defending the land. In June 1944, the Allies finally reached Rome and relieved it.

Rome was often bombed during World War II by both the Allies and the Axis. In total, seventeen bombings of the Eternal City occurred during 1943 and 1944. Many notable buildings were destroyed, its history lost to the war. The bombing of Rome was controversial even during the war, as people were aware that great parts of Roman and European history were being erased. Even though it was neutral, the Vatican couldn't escape the bombings either. Both the Allies and Axis powers tried their best not to hit the pope's city, but the technology of the time wasn't precise enough. The Vatican was bombed only two times, the first in November 1943, when British planes flew over Rome, and the second in March 1944, when the Germans dropped the bomb. During these bombings, Vatican Radio was almost lost.

After World War II, the Italian king abdicated in favor of his son, Umberto II. Umberto was the last king of Italy. In June 1946, a referendum was held, and the people opted for a republic (by 54 percent of the votes cast). Rome might have been on its knees soon after the war, but the city's ruins became a popular sight for American tourists, who were intrigued by its involvement in World War II. Rome offered its new tourists a cheap cost of living, abundant nightlife, and a newly established movie industry. The Eternal City was never defeated. It continued to thrive as the capital of Italy, which was now a republic.

During the 1950s and 1960s, Rome became the center of the fashion and film industry, producing amazing classics such as *La Dolce Vita* ("The Sweet Life"), *Quo Vadis* ("Where Are You Going?"), *Ben-Hur*, and many more. Rome's population started rising, as Italy became more attractive to foreigners. Its Mediterranean way of life comforted the people, who were tired of war and poverty. The first international airport opened in the early

1960s, bringing even more tourists to Rome. When Italy joined the European Union in 1958, Rome became its third most visited city, with over nine million visitors per year. Although it is still under special treatment, the Vatican City attracts at least a quarter of Italy's tourists each year.

Conclusion

There are only two cities in the world with the title "The Eternal City." One is Kyoto, Japan, where the old wooden temples, houses, and shops resisted time. And the other one is Rome, the capital of Italy, which has been continuously inhabited since its foundation in 753 BCE.

Throughout its history, Rome was a target of many conquests and attacks. It stood through the invasion of the Etruscans and the Carthaginians, the Gauls, the Visigoths, the Vandals, the Ostrogoths, the Normans, and the Holy Roman Empire, among other aggressors. Everyone wanted a piece of it. But Rome always thrived, and it is no wonder the city inspired the poets, both the ancient ones and the modern. The first reference to Rome as the Eternal City was found in the writings of the poet Tibullus from the 1ˢᵗ century BCE. In his verses, he names Rome, *Urbs Aeterna* ("Eternal City"). This name was so attractive to the poets of Emperor Augustus that it became a synonym for Rome.

And indeed, even to modern scholars, Rome seems eternal. Like any other city, Rome had its ups and downs, but each time, she would stand up, brush off her bruises, and continue to thrive. It might be under a new ruler, under a new people, a new religion, or even as part of a new kingdom, but the city continued. It only became richer and more sophisticated, attracting people from all over the world.

But what would a city be without its people? Rome gave us many famous individuals that we can proudly call our ancestors, from the ancient poets and historians, such as Virgil and Livy, to the philosopher-emperor Marcus Aurelius. Rome gave us leaders such as Caesar, but it also gave us Constantine the Great and the rulers of the Byzantine Empire that followed. Rome allowed Renaissance artists and thinkers, such as Michelangelo or Leonardo da Vinci, to spread their wings but also gave birth to ruthless dictators, such as Tiberius, Nero, and even Mussolini.

The city of Rome, which is rich in history and myth, is a World Heritage Site, one of enormous value to humanity. Today, the city continues as the seat of the United Nations, as well as the World Food Programme and the famous Cinecittà Studios, which produces many Academy Award-winning marvels of cinema. For Catholics, Rome has been a special place of pilgrimage since medieval times. After all, it is where the pope resides to this day. The most famous wonder of the Vatican is certainly its mysterious library, which, for the most part, remains closed to the public. Rome remains a city of many wonders, and it continues to carve its way into the future, as it always has.

Here's another book by Captivating History that you might like

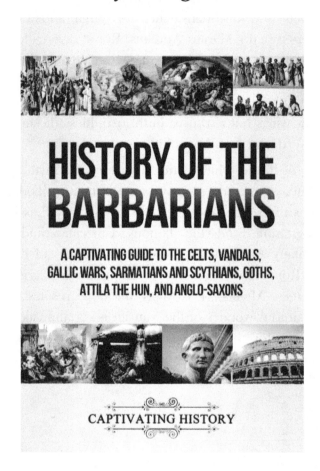

Free Bonus from Captivating History (Available for a Limited time)

Hi History Lovers!

Now you have a chance to join our exclusive history list so you can get your first history ebook for free as well as discounts and a potential to get more history books for free! Simply visit the link below to join.

Captivatinghistory.com/ebook

Also, make sure to follow us on Facebook, Twitter and Youtube by searching for Captivating History.

References

Appian. Roman History. Harvard Univ. Press, 2002.

Arnold, Thomas. History of the Later Roman Commonwealth, from the End of the Second Punic War to the Death of Julius Caesar; and of the Reign of Augustus; with a Life of Trajan. Bickers, 1882.

Cary, M., and H. H. Scullard. "The Temporary Monarchy of Cornelius Sulla." A History of Rome, 1975, pp. 230–238., doi:10.1007/978-1-349-05121-2_23.

Gibbon, Edward, et al. The Decline and Fall of the Roman Empire. Arcturus, 2014.

Gruen, Erich S. "Roman History: Early to Republic." Classics, 2009, doi:10.1093/obo/9780195389661-0023.

Heitland, William Emerton. The Roman Republic. Cambridge University Press, 2014.

Hussey, Joan Mervyn, et al. The Byzantine Empire. Cambridge University Press, 1966.

Keaveney, Arthur. "The Social War." Rome and the Unification of Italy, 2005, pp. 115–162., doi:10.5949/liverpool/9781904675372.003.0003.

Keaveney, Arthur P. "Social War, Roman Republic." The Encyclopedia of Ancient History, 2012, doi:10.1002/9781444338386.wbeah20125.

MILEY, JOHN. HISTORY OF THE PAPAL STATES: from Their Origin to the Present Day (Classic Reprint). FORGOTTEN Books, 2015.

Mommsen, Theodor, and William Purdie Dickson. "The Old Republic and the New Monarchy." The History of Rome, pp. 450–558., doi:10.1017/cbo9780511707544.004.

Morgan, Philip. The Fall of Mussolini: Italy, the Italians, and the Second World War. Oxford University Press, 2008.

Potter, David. "Roman History: Imperial, 31 BCE–284 CE." Classics, 2011, doi:10.1093/obo/9780195389661-0024.

Rose, Herbert Jennings, and John Scheid. "Romulus and Remus." Oxford Research Encyclopedia of Classics, 2016, doi:10.1093/acrefore/9780199381135.013.5610.

Smith, Christopher J. "Romulus and Remus." The Encyclopedia of Ancient History, 2012, doi:10.1002/9781444338386.wbeah20118.

Wilson, Peter H. The Holy Roman Empire: A Thousand Years of Europe's History. Penguin Books, 2017.

Winter, J. M. The Cambridge History of the First World War. Cambridge University Press, 2016.

Made in the USA
Las Vegas, NV
01 October 2023

78424224R00115